D1537894

WAR IN THE GULF

THE SUNDAY TIMES
WAR
IN THE GULF
A PICTORIAL HISTORY

John Witherow & Aidan Sullivan

SIDGWICK & JACKSON
LONDON

Cover photographs Front: An American soldier standing on top of a badly-damaged Iraqi T-62 as Kuwait's oil fields burn at the end of the land war (*Chip Hires/ George Merillon – Gamma/FSP*). Back (upper): The British 7th Armoured Brigade blows up a minefield during live ammunition exercises just before the start of Operation Desert Storm (*Patrick Baz/AFP*). Back (lower): A Kuwaiti holds his son with the backdrop of the Ahmadi oil fields ablaze (*Laurent van der Stockt – Gamma/FSP*)

Title pages: USS *Wisconsin*, the Second World War battleship, firing its 16-inch guns at Iraqi positions on the Kuwaiti coastline. The *Wisconsin*, refitted in the 1980s to enable it to fire Tomahawk cruise missiles, was responsible for destroying the Baath Party headquarters and Ministry of Defence in Baghdad (*Associated Press*)

First published in Great Britain in 1991 by Sidgwick & Jackson Limited

Copyright © 1991 John Witherow and Aidan Sullivan

Designed by Paul Watkins

Graphics and charts by Gordon Beckett and Henry Nolan

Picture research: Candice Temple and Mark Hunt

Text research: Rebecca Fowler

ISBN 0 283 06110 3

Typeset by Pan Macmillan Ltd

Printed by **BPCC Hazell Books**, Aylesbury, Bucks for Sidgwick & Jackson Limited 18–21 Cavaye Place, London SW10 9PG

CONTENTS

THE
RAPE
OF
KUWAIT

Satellite picture of Kuwait City taken on August 15 from a height of 438 miles (AP/Landsat)

Right: Iraqi armour moving through the deserted Salmiya district near the harbour on the first day of the invasion (Sipa/Rex)

Previous pages, left: A mural of Saddam Hussein in Basra against a backdrop of Iraqi military glories from the Iran-Iraq war. As a boy, Saddam had been rejected when he tried to join the army (Sipa/Rex)

Previous pages, right: The first television pictures showing smoke rising from near the Kuwait Towers on the morning of August 2. The towers, one of the city's chief landmarks, are next to Dasman Palace, the home of the emir. Both buildings were damaged, though the towers continued to supply water to parts of the city

THE Kuwaiti border guards knew that something was amiss when they heard a distant rumbling at about 2am on August 2. It was a brilliant, cool night, lit by a bright moon and stars that slid across the sky. Over the featureless desert the Kuwaitis could make out the threatening shapes of a squadron of T-72 tanks thundering towards them followed by an almost luminous cloud of dust. The guards were unsure how to react. Although Saddam Hussein had been steadily increasing the number of troops on the border to 100,000, nobody had expected him to invade.

The engagement was brutally short. The first tanks opened fire at a range of several hundred yards. And while the Kuwaitis put up a token fight with automatic weapons, it was an unequal contest: the Americans were later to describe the invasion as a 'cakewalk'. Within minutes the T-72s – part of a five-pronged attack – were trundling across the border and heading for Kuwait City.

Above them the Iraqi air force's Migs and Mirages had already got to work. One of their first victims was British Airways flight 149 en route to Kuala Lumpur. The pilot was running through pre-flight checks when the international airport came under attack and he had to abandon plans to take off. The Iraqis' objective was to destroy the Kuwaiti air force of fifty-four combat aircraft and helicopters, though most escaped to Saudi Arabia after putting up scant resistance. One Kuwaiti plane was seen to shoot down an Iraqi helicopter before being driven away by ground fire. Elsewhere helicopter-

Right: A home video showing Kuwaiti forces defending the Dasman Palace, the emir's residence, a few hours after Iraqi troops entered Kuwait City. In the bottom right hand corner is the date and time. The Kuwaiti army, hopelessly outnumbered and ill-prepared for the invasion, was quickly overwhelmed by the advancing Republican Guard. Fighting went on for much of the day, but after that resistance came from spasmodic guerrilla attacks (Sipa/Rex)

Opposite: A Young Kuwaiti girl in tears stands outside the Iraq embassy in London holding a picture of the emir, Sheikh Jaber al-Sabah, two days after the invasion. Thousands of Kuwaitis fled the country; a quarter of the 750,000 Kuwaiti population was already abroad (Simon Townsley/ *Sunday Times*)

borne troops seized airports and amphibious landings were made on two disputed islands. It all went as easily as Saddam had predicted to his generals.

The Guards' units which led the invasion had a clear objective: to seal off Kuwait City and trap the ruling al-Sabah family. They did not take account, however, of the telephone, a device which proliferated in a country obsessed with gadgetry. Before long telephones were ringing impatiently, spreading word of Iraqi treachery. Those members of the 1,000 or so ruling al-Sabah clan who were not enjoying the cooler climes of Europe knew they had only one choice: to flee.

After piling valuable papers and souvenirs into armour-plated limousines, a convoy of cars raced south to the safety of Saudi Arabia from Dasman Palace, the emir's seafront residence. Few of the family stayed to fight. One, Sheikh Fahd, a brother of the ruler and the manager of the Kuwaiti national soccer team, chose valour before caution. He was shot on the steps of the palace.

The rest fled. Though not a glorious retreat, it did frustrate Saddam' ambition to round up and parade the al-Sabahs as the 'corrupt emirs of oil'. If they had been

taken, it seemed the Iraqi plan was either to set the emir up as a quisling, or to shoot him.

There was no doubting that the Kuwaiti army was woefully ill prepared and vastly outnumbered. An officer later described how he had called the Ministry of Defence at 9am, when Iraqi units were already in the city, and was told that they had no orders to mobilise. The ministry had already announced that the country had been invaded, adding the immortal lines: 'We did not expect this.'

Later there were to be many bitter recriminations. One Kuwaiti military attaché, who had been in Basra before the invasion, said he had given frequent warnings of an imminent attack which had been ignored. There was, however, some stubborn resistance, with fighting at royal palaces and at main barracks north of the capital. Both came under attack from Iraqi planes and helicopter gunships. To the west of the city, other battles went on all day as hundreds of tanks, armoured personnel carriers and truckloads of troops piled into Kuwait. Residents woke to find the city wrapped in smoke and the air sharp with the smell of cordite. Occasional gunfire and shelling could be heard. One man said he had

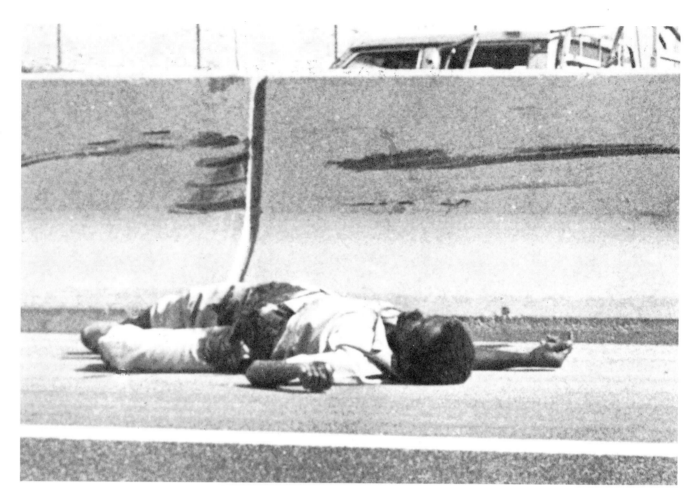

The body of an Iraqi lies in the street in Kuwait City following an attack by the Kuwaiti resistance 16 days after the invasion. The Kuwaitis mounted a dogged guerrilla war until the Iraqis cracked down, using torture and summary executions. As casualties mounted, the resistance was forced to change tactics (Gamma/FSP)

looked down on the American embassy building from a hotel roof: 'I saw the ambassador burning paper, and I knew it was serious.'

For a while there was a surreal sense of normality. People commuted to work blissfully unaware of an invasion, hours after the Iraqis had parked tanks on the corniche. Some thought it was a Kuwaiti army exercise. Many could not believe they could have been invaded by another Arab state; they assumed this was a show of force by Saddam to extort money from the al-Sabahs. The family, however, would have none of it. They appealed by radio for resistance to continue. 'Make the aggressors taste the chalice of death,' implored one al-Sabah . . . 'Citizens, your country is being subjected to a barbaric invasion . . . it is time to defend it.' The radio was silenced within thirty-six hours.

The emir, Sheikh Jaber al-Sabah, had fled in a state of shock at about 5am, just before Iraqi units arrived. He was to end up in Taif, near Mecca, where he led a rather sad existence on the fifth floor of the al-Hada Sheraton hotel surrounded by his government-in-exile and smooth American public relations men. From there

some of the family sought to direct the resistance, much to the irritation of those fighting. 'Ours is like the French exile government of the Second World War', said one of the emir's brothers.

The worst was over in a matter of hours, though throughout the day machine-gun and mortar fire could be heard. Estimates of the number of casualties were unreliable, but scores on both sides were wounded and an unknown number killed. Before long Iraqi soldiers were racing through the city waving their national flag as helicopters hovered overhead. The best units soon moved south to occupy land and deter a counter-attack. Although Saddam may later have toyed with the idea of seizing Saudi Arabia as well, he had no intention yet of taking on the House of Saud. For the moment, he claimed he had been invited in to help overthrow a corrupt regime. Once this was achieved, his troops would pull out. No one believed it; his 'Transitional Free Government' was formed from Iraqis. Their feeble attempt to pass as locals consisted of putting ghutras on their heads to imitate the Gulf Arabs. It was their accents which gave them away.

A Kuwaiti exile shows the United Nations evidence of Iraqi atrocities. He is holding a photograph of a man who had a miraculous escape after he was shot through the back of the head; the bullet came out through his mouth. Evidence of Iraqi atrocities only emerged gradually from Kuwait, but it became clear that the country had been plundered and its people subjected to a terrifying occupation. Thousands died in torture centres set up by the Mukhabarat, the Iraqi secret police. At one, Nayef Palace, tragic last messages were scrawled on the walls by Kuwaitis just as they went to their death (Mark Lennihan/AP)

At first the Iraqis appeared disciplined, with the authorities punishing looting with summary executions. But it did not last. Soon Kuwait City, renowned throughout the Middle East for its enormous opulence, was being pillaged on a scale not seen since the Conquistadores ransacked the Aztec and Inca empires. Within days, soldiers had emptied the gold souk and were scouring shops and houses for anything of value. Officers were cheerfully clambering into limousines, so much a status symbol for Kuwaitis, and driving them off to their barracks. One dealer lost his entire fleet of 4,000 Chevrolets and Oldsmobiles in a day. Even traffic lights, street lamps and the seats from the football stadium were carted off to the north. Entertainment City, the Disneyland of the Gulf and an oasis of American kitsch, was cleaned out. Lorries were seen heading north with the 'space needle', 'atom smasher' and roller coasters for the future amusement of Baghdadis. Iraqi curators, who had long coveted the priceless collections of the emirate, arrived to select the finest art treasures from Kuwait's museums. Even the zoo did not escape the Iraqis' acquisitive eyes. The most exotic animals

were loaded on trucks for the gruelling journey north. The greatest plundering was from the Central Bank, which was emptied of its $1.5 billion in gold and currencies.

Much of the loot was to appear in Baghdad's Shurjah market, where delighted residents were suddenly being offered everything from stuffed olives to French cheeses, delicacies they had not seen for years. Packing cases with Kuwait stamped on the side lay discarded as lorries headed to the capital creaking under loads of food and electrical goods. This sudden shopping bonanza was a pleasant diversion for the Iraqis.

For a while the systematic looting seemed to indicate that Saddam intended to plunder the country before withdrawing. But on August 8 he annexed Kuwait and made it the 19th province of Iraq, calling it Kadhimat. It was now clear that he had no intention of leaving; merely stripping one of the richest cities in the world of its wealth and leaving it as a provincial Iraqi port. It was not long before Saddam's giant portrait – so much a part of everyday life in Iraq – began to appear in the city. By the end of September Kuwaitis had to hand over their

This sequence of pictures shows the execution of six Iraqi soldiers in Kuwait City for looting apartments. Crowds were rounded up and forced to watch the executions, which took place in November. Although the Iraqis systematically plundered Kuwait – stealing an estimated $100 billion worth of assets – they also sought to impose discipline on their own troops. The pictures (right and below) shown the firing squad at work. In the main picture (opposite page), the figure in white is a doctor who had been called to witness the executions and ensure the victims were dead. On examining the bodies, he found one of the men was still alive and summoned an Iraqi officer to administer the *coup de grace* (Ahmed–Sipa/Rex)

The emir of Kuwait, Sheikh Jaber al-Sabah, at a conference in the Saudi seaside city of Jeddah. Behind him and to his left is his cousin, the Crown Prince and prime minister, Sheikh Saad al-Sabah. The al-Sabahs fled *en masse* soon after the invasion, just evading Iraqi troops. From his exile in a luxury hotel in Taif, near Mecca, the emir waited for seven months for the liberation of his country (Gilles Bassignac–Gamma/FSP)

passports, vehicle papers and identity cards. Everything Kuwaiti was being eradicated, even local time. Those who did not change their watches to Iraqi time had them smashed. The currency was merged with Iraq's at a predictably unfavourable rate.

The Kuwaitis and foreigners who had not fled withdrew into their homes, listening to foreign radio broadcasts and agonising over their fate. Theirs was a twilight existence, hiding from house-to-house searches and living on stockpiled food. Iraqis tried to force embassies to move to Baghdad, but most refused and started a celebrated defiance. The few remaining British diplomats, including the ambassador, Michael Weston, survived on a diet of frankfurters and boiled water from the swimming pool.

By September there were still about 1,000 Britons and 1,400 Americans trapped in Kuwait; many were only to escape in December when Saddam agreed that all Westerners could leave. The unlucky ones were hauled off as 'guests' to strategic sites. But their hardship was as nothing when set against the atrocities inflicted on Kuwaitis. Those fleeing across the border brought tales of rape, torture, murder and execution. At

first the stories seemed incredible. Only after the liberation of Kuwait did the true horror emerge.

The sudden brutality was in part a response to the resistance, who were more stubborn than the Iraqis had expected, carrying out bombing and machinegun attacks. Shots could often be heard in the early hours and at dusk – dubbed 'Rambo hour'. At night they shouted anti-Iraqi slogans from rooftops and daubed the town with graffiti. A favourite was: 'Saddam lives here', scrawled on rubbish bins. At its peak the resistance was killing or wounding twenty-five Iraqis a day, despite being under-armed and ill-organised.

The man given responsibility for dealing with this irritant was Ali Hassan al-Majid, the governor, a cousin of Saddam who had earned his spurs gassing 5,000 Kurds in 1988. Al-Majid in turn employed the Mukhabarat, the Iraqi secret police which had ruthlessly eradicated opposition to Saddam at home. Up to 7,000 of them moved into the city and began systematically to decimate the resistance. They set up torture chambers in schools and at the Nayef Palace, headquarters of the Kuwaiti police. From there they embarked on an orgy of punishment. By October an estimated 1,200 resistance fighters had been killed and by the time of the liberation possibly 5,000. There were so many bodies that an ice-skating rink had to be turned into a morgue.

The tactics were well-known to anyone familiar with the atrocities of the Second World War. One witness said they were 'catching men and young boys and putting them in front of their houses and shooting them. They hand their mothers or wives a paper saying: "We have killed your husband and your son because we think this person was one of the Kuwaiti resistance – which does not exist".'

Being found with a picture of the emir was enough to ensure the burning of homes; possession of a gun meant death. A supermarket manager was killed for refusing to display a picture of Saddam after he had his fingers cut off, his right arm broken and his face burned with cigarettes. At first the Iraqis tolerated some demonstrations by women carrying portraits of the emir. But that changed when they began to shout 'Death to Saddam'. Women became the victims of regular assaults. Indians, Pakistanis, Filipinos and Kuwaitis all fell victim to casual rapes. There were other horrific tales of women taken into captivity and raped repeatedly before being murdered.

Torture became commonplace, including electric shock and systematic beatings. Fingernails were torn off and eyes gouged out. Nayef Palace was the scene of some of the worst horrors, but there were other places, such as the Qasma athletic stadium, where women were killed in the changing rooms. At Nayef, tragic messages were found scrawled on walls: 'Goodbye. This is my last night,' said one. Another in English said: 'I love my lover Naseema. I love her with my hert (sic) and never forget her.'

The reign of terror inevitably had an effect on the resistance. If they killed an Iraqi, five Kuwaitis would be murdered in retribution. 'It was getting to the point where children were being shot in front of their parents,' said a resistance man. One fighter was crucified before he was shot.

Another was caught with a letter he was writing to President Bush appealing for help, and was shot in the head and left in the street with the letter still in his hand. Eventually they had no choice but to change tactics, resorting to passive resistance. This involved clothing and feeding fellow Kuwaitis, collecting information on Iraqi military deployments to transmit to Riyadh and risking their lives helping foreigners. The Iraqis had long been renowned throughout the Arab world as thugs. But as the stories of barbarism began to filter out, it became apparent that this was a regime that would have to be driven, not cajoled, out of Kuwait.

Left: George Bush knew this was the biggest crisis of his presidency, and he immediately set out to pursue a twin-track approach: a military buildup to persuade Saddam to retreat from Kuwait and if necessary force him out; and a diplomatic offensive that would isolate Iraq and encourage it to leave voluntarily. His main instrument of policy was the telephone, and he is shown here speaking to an aide from his golf buggy at his east coast holiday home at Kennebunkport. The telephone was vital to him in getting enough support for tough UN sanctions and to form an extraordinary 28-nation military coalition (Jim Bourg/Reuter)

Below: As the shock of the invasion reverberated around the world, King Fahd of Saudi Arabia became a key player. He knew Saddam now threatened his own existence, and thus agreed to cut an Iraqi oil pipeline which ran through the kingdom and invite in hundreds of thousands of non-Muslims to a country regarded as the shrine of Islam. Fahd, aware this might cause internal tensions, favoured a rapid transition to war (Press Association)

A LINE
IN THE
SAND

Above: An American sailor bids an emotional farewell as he prepares to board the aircraft carrier, the USS *Theodore Roosevelt* (Adrian Snider–Sipa/Rex)

Right: Some of the first US Marines leaving for the Gulf from Mayport naval station, Florida, on August 7. The United States deployed 80,000 Marines to the region (Gamma/FSP)

Previous pages, left: US troops heading for the Gulf boarding a 747 (Miller/Colorific)

Previous pages, right: British soldiers wave farewell en route to Saudi Arabia (Press Association)

GEORGE BUSH was relaxing in his private quarters on the second floor of the White House just before 9pm when his friend and national security adviser, Brent Scowcroft, burst in with the news that Iraqi troops had crossed the border two hours earlier and were about to take Kuwait City.

It came as much as a surprise to the president as it did to the Kuwaitis. Although he had a CIA report which stated that an invasion was likely, the consensus in the intelligence world was that it was a bluff. They believed that Saddam Hussein was after limited objectives – better access to the Gulf, oil from a disputed field and the wiping out of debts to Kuwait. He could achieve that by threats. Saddam, they reasoned, might be a bully, but he was not a fool. He was also an ally of sorts and a bulwark against the spread of Islamic fundamentalism from revolutionary Iran.

Ally or not, the president knew he had a crisis on his hands. He immediately convened a top-level meeting in the White House Situation Room to consider the options. The military ones were not encouraging. Kuwait was 9,000 miles away and the United States had no bases in the area. It was obvious it would be a huge operation getting enough troops there to eject Saddam. One aide said they would need 90,000 men, a number that at the time seemed vast. Even then, the Americans marvelled at the size of Saddam's armed forces: one million men and 5,500 tanks. An amateur historian

Ship of the Desert: The bow of the USS *America* seems to carve its way through the desert as it heads down the Suez Canal to take up position in the Red Sea. On the flight deck is an F-14 Tomcat. By the time the air war started, the United States had six carrier battle groups in the region, the biggest gathering of naval air power since the Second World War. With F/A-18 Hornets, F-14 Tomcats, A-6 Intruders, E-2C Hawkeyes and 6-EA Prowlers, the carriers were able to contribute 360 aircraft to the raids on Iraq (Nelson-AFP/ Popperfoto)

pointed out to the president that Iraq had more armour than both sides in North Africa during the Second World War. It was, he added, the fourth largest army in the world.

More alarming, there were signs that Saddam might move on Saudi Arabia, enabling Iraq to control one third of the world's oil supply. America knew that such domination by a man like Saddam could force up oil prices and plunge the global economy deeper into recession. The choice was between acting now, or facing a more formidable opponent in the future. Bush was well aware of Iraq's long search for a nuclear bomb and Saddam's fascination with bizarre weapons, such as a long-range supergun. The president asked the Chiefs of Staff to draw up a plan to prevent such an invasion. Saddam had to be stopped now.

With the military options looking bleak, Bush turned to consider other means. Economic sanctions seemed the best bet. Though their track record was poor, Scowcroft pointed out that Iraq was especially vulnerable because of its reliance on oil exports and on imports of essential products, including weaponry. That was fine, said Bush, but how could he enforce such an embargo, and how would the Arabs react to an economic stranglehold on one of their neighbours? Bush went to bed in a troubled mood, aware that he was almost certainly facing the biggest test of his presidency. He was not to get much rest; Scowcroft woke him at 5am to sign two directives freezing Iraq's assets in the United States and banning trade with the aggressor. As he did so, senior defence department officials were meeting to consider in detail the military options.

The Pentagon knew that if Saddam moved south to the Saudi oilfields they had only one option: air power. Warplanes could strike from carriers or friendly countries, while giant B-52s could fly from the Indian Ocean island of Diego Garcia to hit invading ground forces. But that would not shift Saddam's occupying army and it would endanger the lives of thousands of Americans working in Iraq and Kuwait. Bush was well aware of how the Iranian hostage crisis had paralysed the administration of Jimmy Carter in 1979. The Pentagon, however, did have an off-the-shelf plan for reinforcing the area in the event of a crisis, and that was put into effect. Aircraft carrier battle groups were diverted to the region and rapid deployment forces – such as the 82nd Airborne – put on alert. Colin Powell, chairman of the Joint Chiefs of Staff, persuaded Bush that if he was going to commit American troops, he would have to do it quickly and on a massive scale. Powell was a Vietnam veteran, and like many others in the conflict, he was determined to avoid the mistakes of that war. This would mean fast and overwhelming

Right: President Hosni Mubarak and King Fahd meeting in Jeddah just days before the invasion of Kuwait. Saddam Hussein had assured both leaders that he had no intention of invading. This betrayal encouraged them to forge an alliance with the United States and created a new power structure in the region (Reuter)

Centre: George Bush and Margaret Thatcher met within days of the invasion at the Aspen, Colorado, home of Henry Catto, the US ambassador to London. Both pledged to take all necessary action to force Saddam to withdraw. The war was to reinforce Britain's fading 'special relationship' with the United States (Malcolm Clarke/*Sunday Times*)

Below: The crisis also led to the fracturing of old friendships. The relationship between George Bush and King Hussein of Jordan, long seen as an ally in the region, cooled abruptly as the king sought to play a mediating role with Saddam Hussein (Reuter)

Far right, above: One of Bush's prime objectives was to secure the support of President Mikhail Gorbachev. This he achieved at the Helsinki summit on September 9 when they agreed a policy over United Nations sanctions (Reuter)

Far right, below: Bush was to give immediate support to the ousted emir, despite some concerns in the United States that he was supporting an autocratic leader. The emir eased such worries by pledging $15 billion to the United States (Associated Press)

action without political interference. The president agreed. He was to pledge that this would 'not be another Vietnam'.

As part of his twin-track policy, Bush set to work to enforce his economic war against Saddam and prepare the ground for military deployments. The telephone was to be his main instrument of policy, and over the next few months there was scarcely a president, king or prime minister who did not have George Bush on the line at regular intervals. It became so vital that the president used it from his golf buggy and his speedboat at his holiday home at Kennebunkport.

His first aim was to cut Iraq's oil exports, and one of his first calls was to King Fahd of Saudi Arabia from Air Force One as he flew to Colorado to meet Margaret Thatcher. An Iraqi pipeline ran through the kingdom and it was essential that this, together with one through Turkey, should be cut. Fahd was sympathetic, though cautious. He feared such a move could provoke an Iraqi invasion. Perhaps inevitably, the firmest support came from Mrs Thatcher, who cared more for Britain's special relationship with the United States that for its ties with continental Europe. She quickly agreed to send Royal Air Force planes, and as the crisis developed began to regard herself an honorary member of the Washington war cabinet. Bush later recalled that she told him: 'Remember George, this is no time to go wobbly.'

Bush was far from wobbly. But all the Americans could do at this stage was to look and sound warlike. The president moved swiftly to the United Nations. As a former ambassador there, he knew just how irresolute it could be. But he also knew that he needed its backing if he was to secure effective sanctions against Iraq. He had the difficult job of appearing decisive at home, while persuading the world community to follow his lead. The allied triumph at the UN – over the next four months they were to get eleven key resolutions passed – was a vital factor in eventual success.

The first week was the most critical of the Bush presidency. He knew he was facing decisions similar to those which confronted Harry Truman over Korea and Jack Kennedy over Vietnam. He also knew he was about to commit US power to the most dangerous region in the world – where America's influence had been constantly frustrated – and into a crisis whose outcome was far from clear.

The first triumph of his 'speed-dialling' diplomacy came when Fahd agreed to allow American troops to deploy to the kingdom. It was a difficult decision for a man who regarded himself as the custodian of the holy cities of Medina and Mecca. But ultimately he had little choice. Even if Saddam did not invade, failure to eject him from Kuwait would whet his appetite for further

25

About 300 Apache AH-64s – known as the Dragonflies of Death – were deployed for Operation Desert Storm. Despite initial concerns over their reliability, they were to prove a success in destroying large numbers of Iraqi tanks and APCs. The aircraft has a crew of two and can cruise at 180mph, often hunting for targets in groups of 20 or more. Armed with 16 laser-guided Hellfire missiles, 76 70mm rockets and a 30mm Chain Gun Cannon, they are regarded as one of the most effective tank killers in the world. The helicopters are equipped with TADS (target acquisition and designation sight), which magnifies targets at ranges of several miles, and PNVS (pilot night vision sensor), which produces a passive thermal image of the world outside the cockpit on a helmet-mounted display (Alain Arnoult/Impact)

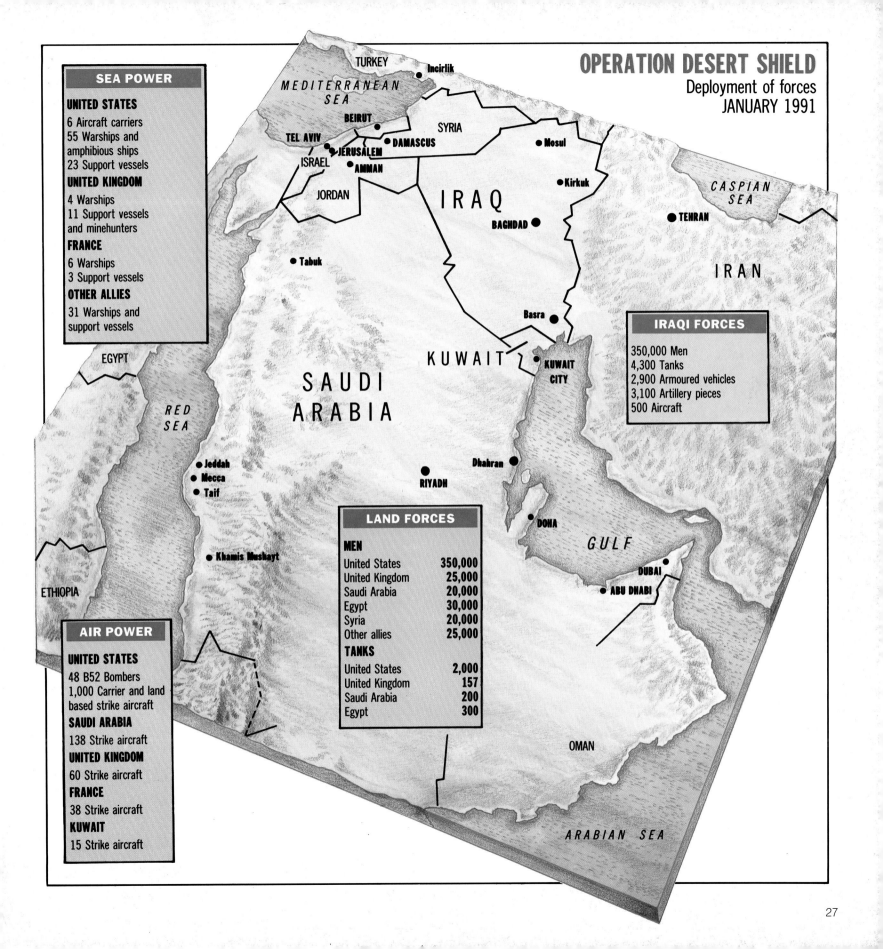

OPERATION DESERT SHIELD
Deployment of forces
JANUARY 1991

SEA POWER

UNITED STATES
6 Aircraft carriers
55 Warships and
amphibious ships
23 Support vessels

UNITED KINGDOM
4 Warships
11 Support vessels
and minehunters

FRANCE
6 Warships
3 Support vessels

OTHER ALLIES
31 Warships and
support vessels

IRAQI FORCES
350,000 Men
4,300 Tanks
2,900 Armoured vehicles
3,100 Artillery pieces
500 Aircraft

LAND FORCES

MEN

United States	350,000
United Kingdom	25,000
Saudi Arabia	20,000
Egypt	30,000
Syria	20,000
Other allies	25,000

TANKS

United States	2,000
United Kingdom	157
Saudi Arabia	200
Egypt	300

AIR POWER

UNITED STATES
48 B52 Bombers
1,000 Carrier and land
based strike aircraft

SAUDI ARABIA
138 Strike aircraft

UNITED KINGDOM
60 Strike aircraft

FRANCE
38 Strike aircraft

KUWAIT
15 Strike aircraft

TURKEY
Incirlik
MEDITERRANEAN SEA
BEIRUT
SYRIA
TEL AVIV
DAMASCUS
JERUSALEM
Mosul
ISRAEL
AMMAN
JORDAN
IRAQ
Kirkuk
CASPIAN SEA
BAGHDAD
TEHRAN
Tabuk
IRAN
Basra
KUWAIT
KUWAIT CITY
SAUDI ARABIA
RED SEA
EGYPT
Jeddah
Mecca
Dhahran
Taif
RIYADH
DOHA
GULF
Khamis Mushayt
DUBAI
ETHIOPIA
ABU DHABI
OMAN
ARABIAN SEA

27

The searing desert heat was to be a constant burden for the troops in the first months of buildup. T.E. Lawrence described how the 'heat of Arabia came out like a drawn sword and struck us speechless.'

Left: A US Marine from the 7th Expeditionary Brigade feeling the heat in the Saudi desert after a chemical warfare protection exercise. When they arrived in August, temperatures were as high as 40°C (AFP/Popperfoto)

Opposite above (left): Water was a constant problem for the allied forces. During the summer each soldier was meant to drink a staggering 40 litres a day (Sipa/Rex)

Opposite above (right): A trooper with the 24th Infantry Division displays his tattoo (Delahaye–Sipa/Rex)

Opposite below: US Marines from the First Reconnaissance Battalion keeping fit and cool by running down a beach in Saudi Arabia (Philippe Wojazer/Reuter)

Women at war: The United States deployed 33,000 women in Saudi Arabia, some of them near the front line. One American woman was taken captive by the Iraqis. Their presence was to cause problems for strict Saudi society, where women were expected to stay out of sight.

Below left: Mike Moore/ *Today*; Centre top: Eric Bouvet–Gamma/FSP; Centre bottom: Andy Clarke/DOD pool; Opposite: Dennis Brack– Black Star/ Colorific

conquest and jeopardise the future of the House of Saud. Within days the All Americans – the 82nd Airborne – were in Saudi Arabia and digging in near the border. Although it was to be several weeks before the United States had enough troops effectively to defend the kingdom, and seven months before there were sufficient to invade Kuwait and Iraq, Bush had 'drawn a line in the sand.'

At first the Americans were only admitting plans to deploy up to 100,000 troops. But in reality they were intending to get quarter of a million forces into the region as quickly as possible. Even then there were fears this would not be enough. And so began a steady buildup by both sides; by the time war broke out the allies had 650,000 servicemen and women in the region

confronting hundreds of thousands of Iraqis across the desert.

Fahd also agreed – as did President Turgut Ozal of Turkey – to cut Iraqi oil exports. Bush was now beginning to make progress, forging a grand alliance by securing the support of half a dozen Western allies and the Arab League, including Egypt. Arab support was vital for ensuring this was not seen as a neo-colonial war. Britain had begun sending Tornado and Jaguar aircraft, and soon an extraordinary coalition of twenty-eight nations – embracing everyone from the Senegalese to Mujahadeen guerrillas – was scrambling to dispatch troops to Saudi Arabia. In early September Mrs Thatcher and her war cabinet decided to send the 7th Armoured Brigade from Germany. That was later

followed by the 4th Armoured Brigade, making the British presence second only to that of the United States among the Western allies.

The crisis meant an immediate international realignment, with old alliances falling apart and new ones being formed. The Syrians, for long Soviet allies, were soon dug in alongside American and British troops. Even France, ever the odd man out, sent a carrier and dispatched some of their finest units to the desert, including the Foreign Legion. President François Mitterrand was one of the first to speak of the 'logic of war', though his defence minister, Jean-Pierre Chevenement, a founder member of the Franco-Iraqi friendship club, was clearly loath to take any military action against an erstwhile ally. As a result France's role appeared ambivalent; while talking of war Mitterrand sent 'Twelve Apostles' around the Middle East to explain his sympathetic posture to Arab countries.

Elsewhere support was mixed. Surprisingly, the Soviet Union was bullish. Bush was well aware that had it not been for the end of the Cold War, such an invasion could have precipitated a superpower crisis; thus one of his prime objectives was to get Mikhail Gorbachev on board. He appeared to have achieved this in the United Nations and at a summit in Helsinki, where the Russians had been co-operative, handing over valuable intelligence about the Iraqi military machine which they had done so much to construct. But old superpower suspicions remained, and there were questions about the role of hundreds of Soviet military advisers still in Iraq,

The danger that Saddam would use chemical weapons was a constant fear of allied forces. He had used nerve gas against the Kurds in 1988 and mustard gas during the Iran-Iraq war. He was also known to be developing biological weapons. Allied forces routinely underwent training against chemical weapons and wore their special suits into battle.

Left: Ozturk-Sipa/Rex; below and opposite: Abbas/Magnum

A diverse coalition of nations began to mass their troops in the Saudi desert from late summer, 1990. Apart from the Americans, the British sent the 1st Armoured Division from Germany, the Egyptians dispatched 35,000 troops and the Syrians 19,000. The French also sent the Foreign Legion and the armoured Daguet Division. The Saudis deployed 40,000 men, the second biggest force after the United States. Scattered among them were troops from, among others, Senegal, Bangladesh, Pakistan, Czechoslovakia and New Zealand. Even the Afghan Mujahadeen sent guerrillas to advise the allies on how to deal with Soviet weapons.

Right: Saudi troops unload from the cargo ship *Saudi Qassim* to join other Arab defence forces (Diether Endlicher)

Below: A French trooper of the 1st Combat Helicopter Regiment with a Puma behind him. Many troops used scarves or the Arabic ghutra to protect their faces from the desert sand storms (Gilles Bassignac–Gamma/FSP)

Saudi troops positioned on the border with Kuwait. The Saudis were to play an important role in the battle for Khafji, the first big ground engagement of the war, when the Iraqis launched an incursion into Saudi territory. The town was eventually retaken after intensive fighting (Tom Stoddard/Katz)

Below: The Kuwaitis were determinded to play a part in the struggle to regain their homeland, and contributed thousands of men to the 10,000-strong Gulf Cooperation Council forces. A training officer is standing on the chest of a Kuwaiti army volunteer as part of the toughening up exercises for the battle ahead (Russell Boyce/Reuter)

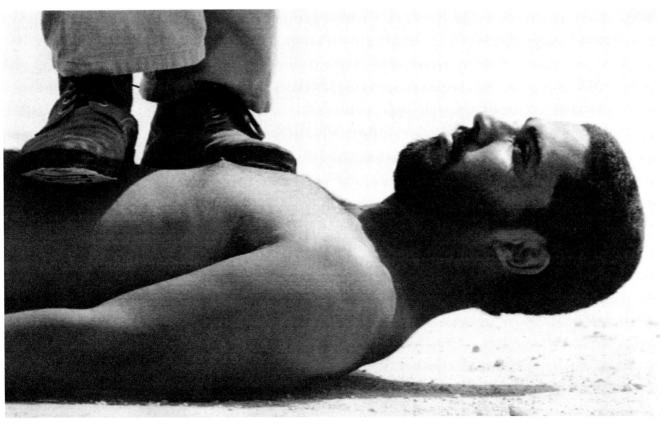

George Bush went to
Saudia Arabia to spend
Thanksgiving with
American forces. He is
seen here throwing
tie-clips to US soldiers
(Diana Walker-Gamma/
FSP; a winner in the world
press photo competition,
1991)

Saddam visited his troops in Kuwait just before the expiry of the January 15 United Nations deadline. He joked that the Americans would not dare come, and if they did his men would defeat them in 'the mother of all battles'. Saddam later visited the forces again during the air war, and just escaped being killed when his convoy came under attack from two American F-16s. Only after weeks of relentless bombing did he consider a withdrawal. But by then it was regarded by the allies as 'too little, too late' (INA/Reuter)

and initial Soviet reluctance to enforce a military block-ade. Gorbachev, too, was preoccupied with a deteriorating situation at home; this made him reluctant to antagonise the old guard and the military. These men, children of the Cold War, feared that the United States would crush Iraq and dominate the region for years to come. Aware of this, the White House was patient, assuming that Gorbachev was under intense pressure from his generals not to ditch Saddam. In the end, fears of Soviet double-dealing were unfounded, and Moscow proved that it had come of age in the new order.

Most disappointing from the allies' point of view was the role of Japan and newly-united Germany. Japan vacillated, debating endlessly how much money to contribute in between sending Sony Walkmans to the soldiers in the desert. And Germany, despite being the richest country in Europe with one of the best armies and air forces, refused to get involved. Although Chancellor Helmut Kohl was sympathetic to the allied requests, his hands were tied by a coalition government and a people who had a deeply-ingrained loathing of confrontation after their role in the Second World War.

Their attitude, however, was far from universal. Although early American opinion polls showed a reluctance to go to war to restore an autocratic emir to his luxurious lifestyle, Saddam's intransigent behaviour soon changed that. The polls there and in Britain showed a singleminded determination to remove Saddam from Kuwait – and even from power – at almost any cost. The debate in the United States about the ethics of the war was more heated than in Britain, where people seemed to know a ruthless dictator when they saw one.

Because of the dangers, and because he relished such drama, Bush became totally absorbed in the crisis, largely ignoring domestic policy. 'His attitude,' said one senior Republican, 'was that his presidency was on the line, so he was going to make darn sure that he was in charge.' Despite rather laboured efforts to look relaxed, his day was dominated by events in the Gulf. When he was at Kennebunkport, he would call the senior duty officer each morning at 5.45am in the Situation Room to get the latest news.Then he would meet his small group of advisers to review progress. Their main worry was convincing Saddam that they meant business, and that the buildup was going faster than it actually was. While the United States claimed to have deployed large numbers of troops, in fact only parts of units were sent, and it was to be some time before there were enough allied forces to repel an invasion. If Saddam had pushed south without delay, he could have seized Saudi Arabia and left the West floundering.

Saddam, however, seemed to have no such ambitions, at least for the present. He was content to annex and plunder Kuwait. He told the American chargé d'affaires he would not budge, and one senior US official said his mood could be summed up as: 'Go do something about it, baby'. The Iraqi propaganda machine was already preparing the country for the 'mother of all battles'. Saddam said he would 'turn Iraqi territory into a cemetery with no tombstones for aggressors.' Hyperbole was to be a feature of the crisis; Saddam bragged to interlocutors that he did not know what the fuss was about and that he could survive any siege. It was another example of how he had misjudged the changing global order. Saddam's defiant boast that the allies would need twelve million soldiers to defeat his army was merely seen as more Baghdad bombast. Taking its cue from such statements, the Ministry of Information warned that Iraqis would eat American pilots who were shot down.

The rhetoric struck a chord in the radical Arab world. Whatever their leaders were saying or doing, many Arabs saw Saddam as a new Saladin who would go on to destroy Israel and free them from Western domination. This support was especially strong in Jordan, with its big Palestinian community, where the Iraqi president became a hero. Saddam had cleverly manipulated

Much of the soldiers' time in the desert, when they were not training, was devoted to relaxation and keeping clean. Some whiled away the hours with scorpion fights, playing basketball or poker, and writing letters. Some even developed a new dance called the 'Gas mask'. They tried to celebrate Christian festivals out of sight of the strictly-Islamic Saudis.

Left: Christmas in the Gulf: an American officer dresses up rather half-heartedly as Father Christmas (Peter Turnley–Black Star/Colorific)

Below: A British soldier, Lifeguard Trooper Mark Doyle, aged 21, takes an improvised shower (Mike Moore/*Today*)

Opposite: Some found animals to adopt. Here a soldier from the 4th Armoured Brigade looks after a stray puppy (Mike Moore/*Today*)

Arab prejudices agains the 'rich, indolent and uncultured' Gulf Arabs. Their vast wealth, said Saddam, should be shared more evenly throughout the Arab world, omitting to mention that he had squandered his own riches on weaponry and war. For the leader of a secular state which until then had little truck with Islam, he brashly played the religious card, accusing the 'evil and corrupt' Saudi royal family of inviting the devil in to protect the holy cities.

As the crisis unfolded, an element of personal animosity crept into the long-distance relationship between Bush and Saddam, which was largely conducted through the 24-hour-a-day Cable News Network. Saddam described Bush as 'the Devil in the White House', and Bush often likened Saddam to Hitler, drawing comparisons with the dangers of appeasement in the 1930s. 'He doesn't want to become another Neville Chamberlain,' said one aide. Bush was concerned there had already been an element of appeasement at a meeting with Saddam just before the invasion when the US ambassador to Baghdad, April Glaspie, did not warn him strongly enough against coveting Kuwait. He was not going to repeat the mistake. The CIA had told him that Saddam suffered from 'malignant narcissism', a dangerous cocktail of arrogance and ambition, and he started to regard his adversary with bewildered contempt.

The allies soon realised that a critical element in forcing Saddam out of Kuwait was convincing him that he faced overwhelming firepower. The military buildup in Saudi Arabia was extraordinary by any standards. Superlatives soon became redundant as it overtook the Berlin airlift of 1948 and the deployments to Korea and Vietnam. Only the American involvement in the Second World War remained unsurpassed. By the end of August the materiel in Saudi Arabia or en route was graphically described by one official as equivalent in weight to 400,000 Chevrolets. Hundreds of aircraft and ships were criss-crossing the globe carrying everything from Coca-Cola to tanks. By the time the war started, allied planes and ships had covered 58 million miles in preparing Desert Shield. It was a statistician's dream. The United States was serving one million meals and delivering 700 tons of mail every day. Into Saudi Arabia flooded all the necessities of modern life: 551,000 bottles of sunscreen lotion; 715,000 cans of footpowder. The British pumped in 150 million pounds of freight and 60,000 tonnes of ammunition. Across America stores were being emptied. The aircraft carrier *John F. Kennedy* alone took on board 22,000 tons of food and 3.5 million gallons of diesel fuel.

The navy presence, too, was formidable. Bush had dispatched four carrier battle groups and had a total of

Major Alistair Wicks of the 14/20th King's Hussars – part of the 4th Armoured Brigade – leads his Challenger tanks to take up front-line positions
(Mike Moore/*Today*)

Left above: An Americ
soldier wearing his NE
outfit trains for the lan
assault (Christopher
Morris–Black Star/
Colorific)

Left below: Three Briti
officers of the 7th
Armoured Brigade wa
live ammunition trainin
(Patrick Baz–AFP/
Popperfoto)

Below: Engineers from
7th Armoured Brigade
blow up a minefield sh
before the start of the
war (Patrick Baz–AFP/
Popperfoto)

thirty-seven warships in the region or en route. In all about seventy ships from eleven countries were moving towards the Gulf. Soon they were intercepting or landing troops on ships that were suspected of breaking the embargo. There were fears that a clash at sea could begin the conflict, or even that the Americans were looking for a pretext for unleashing their military might. By the time war broke out, more than 100 warships were in the region. And though only a few thousand men had arrived on the ground by September, tens of thousands more were on their way. Backing them were the hundreds of warplanes based on the carriers and newly- arrived in Saudi Arabia. Within weeks the United States – together with Britain and Saudi Arabia – was able to match Saddam's 500-strong airforce. The open door to Saudi Arabia had been slammed shut.

One factor governing Western thinking throughout the crisis was time. Once they had deployed enough defensive forces, reaching the magic 'critical mass', the allies could turn again to sanctions as a means of enforcing UN resolutions. Views about this were mixed. Sceptics pointed to the failure of sanctions against South Africa and Rhodesia. But the embargo of Iraq was extraordinary in its thoroughness. Iraqi oil exports had been severed, and only a trickle of food and machinery was getting through. At first it was thought sanctions would begin to bite within weeks, but as time went on it appeared that Iraq was capable of surviving for months, even years. After the war with Iran, Iraqis were used to privation. It was decided to wait until November to see if sanctions were working, but privately the administration was preparing, and even resigning itself, to go to war.

An underlying factor was concern over the cohesion of the coalition. Many expressed fears that it would unravel as tensions increased in the region, that the Saudis would panic and the Egyptians come under domestic pressure to pull out. Some worried about the American public; whether its attention span could tolerate a long siege, and how long the American troops could sit it out in the desert. There was already grumbling, with the soldiers getting bored holding scorpion fights and painting names like 'Scum Dog' on their tanks. The delay allowed time for complaints to emerge about the proportionately larger numbers of blacks and working class Americans in the army. No one relished the thought of the crisis dragging on into another Saudi summer.

Bush was getting conflicting advice from doves and hawks, both inside and outside the administration. Ironically, the most violent doves were the right-wing isolationists who argued that Americans 'don't die for princes, sultans or emirs'. In the opposite corner was

US troops of the 1st Cavalry Division file out across the desert after being addressed by James Baker, the US secretary of state, on a visit to Saudi Arabia (Greg English/AP)

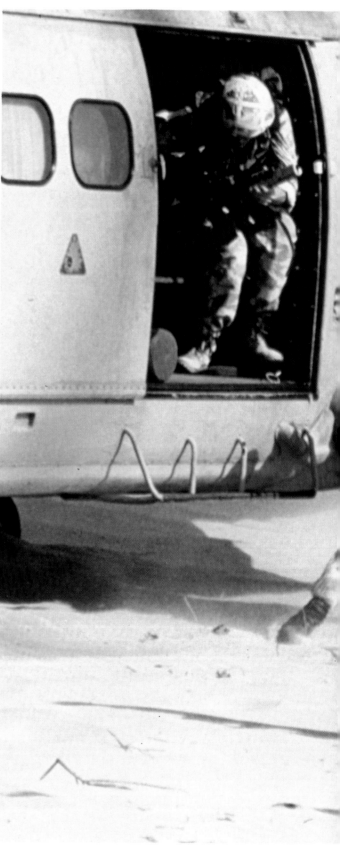

Christopher Morris–Black Star/Colorific

British soldiers from the 1st Staffordshires leap from a Puma helicopter during exercises (Patrick Baz–AFP/Popperfoto)

The United States used the A-10 Thunderbolt as a prime means of attacking Iraqi armour. Slow-moving and ugly, it was known affectionately as the Warthog. The aircraft is armed with six Maverick anti-tank missiles and a 30mm Gatling gun which fires armour-piercing rounds at the rate of 4,000 a minute. Together with the Apache helicopters, it was the allies' main airborne tankbuster. The pilot and sensitive flight controls are protected by titanium armour-plating. The aircraft was to have considerable success during the war, although it was also responsible for some notorious 'own goals', including an attack on British armoured personnnel carriers in which nine soldiers died (Christopher Morris–Black Star/Colorific)

Henry Kissinger, the former secretary of state, who knew a thing or two about military strikes after masterminding the carpet bombing of Cambodia during the early 1970s. He became the patron saint of hawks. As Bush listened to these conflicting voices, there was an undercurrent of anxiety that the Americans would be left stranded while the foundations of the alliance eroded. For a while in October, Bush and the alliance seemed to have lost their way, and it appeared that the president might blink first. In fact few such signs emerged. But it did mean that the Egyptians and the Saudis, who potentially faced the biggest internal unrest, were among the more impatient of the allies, constantly urging the United States to resort to military means.

At one time there was much speculation that the Americans were considering a pre-emptive strike, possibly in retaliation for hostage-taking and to short-circuit a peace deal that would leave Saddam's armies intact. But as Iraqis flooded into Kuwait and began digging in, that option receded. By the autumn the overall American plan of attack was already far advanced. The intention was to get half a million men, together with thousands of tanks, to the region by the New Year to match Iraqi forces.

It was at this time that the West had to consider the 'nightmare scenario'. There were two versions of this: that Saddam might withdraw partially and start negotiating with the less determined Arab partners; or that he would withdraw completely and park his huge army on the border with Kuwait. Some Arab states were even mooting a UN peacekeeping force. It was an unappealing prospect. UN resolutions only demanded that he pull out and pay reparations. They did not set terms for a peace. Privately, many in the administration hoped that he would not prove so sensible; their aim was to destroy Iraq's military night and remove the threat it posed to the Middle East. Saddam, blinkered in his vision of the Iran-Iraq war when he held on for eight years against a numerically-superior enemy, believed he could win a war with the allies. Even before he invaded Kuwait he boasted to the American ambassador that the United States could not tolerate thousands of dead in battle. Quoting Vietnam, he thought they lacked the stomach for a fight.

Certainly the West was unsure how unorthodox an

American M1A1 Abrams tanks power through the desert. The tank was regarded as one of the finest in the world, matched only by the German Leopard II. Fitted with a 1,500 horsepower gas turbine engine and armed with a 120mm gun, its speed and firepower were formidable, though at times its huge fuel consumption created supply problems. About 2,000 of the M1A1s were deployed to the desert. The tank is fitted with a special stabilising sighting system which enables the gunner to keep a target in his sights however rough the terrain. In one engagement it struck a T-72 tank at such a distance that the Iraqi tank commander refused to believe he had been hit by the M1A1, insisting an aircraft was responsible (Peter Turnley–Black Star/ Colorific)

The French aircraft carrier, the *Clemenceau*, aroused much interest when it was deployed to the region carrying only helicopters. The *Clemenceau*, of 1960s vintage and capable of carrying 16 Super Etendards and 1,600 men, was to return to France to collect warplanes (Eric Bouvet-Gamma/FSP)

Overleaf: A Stealth F117 refuels over the Gulf. Designed to have as few radar-reflecting edges as possible and covered in wave-absorbing paint, the Stealth is virtually invisible to radar. The United States deployed about 40 of the $100 million planes to Saudi Arabia. Although slow and not heavily armed, its 'stealthy' capability allowed it to loiter over targets for long periods and use laser-guided weapons with great accuracy. It needed no fighter escort and the USAF estimated one Stealth was worth about nine ordinary aircraft. The Stealth was the first aircraft to attack command and control centres and Scud positions when the air war started (Katz Pictures)

adversary Iraq would prove. Baghdad had become a sanctuary for some of the more ferocious terrorists in the Middle East, and there were reports that they were planning all kinds of mayhem. It was also well known that Saddam intended to drag Israel into any war – he had threatened to incinerate 'the Zionist entity' – and there was much debate about whether he could deliver poison gas and biological weapons using his ballistic missiles. The Americans became convinced that he could produce the virulent anthrax disease, and it was known that he had no scruples about using gas against his own troublesome subjects. Most important of all, Iraq had been striving to produce nuclear weapons. The Israelis had set this programme back for several years when they bombed the Osirak nuclear reactor in Iraq in 1981. But the project was now back on course and no one was sure how close he was to getting the bomb. Some in the administration believed it was only a matter of months, a factor that began to prey on George Bush's mind as he contemplated whether to give sanctions more time to work.

It was a determination to prevent the crisis dragging on indefinitely which led Bush to seek a deadline to force Saddam's hand. He achieved this at the United Nations at the end of November, when the security council passed resolution 678 setting a date of January 15 for Iraqi withdrawal. It was now accepted that the world community did not have the patience to wait for sanctions to erode Iraq's will. But it was prepared to give him, 'as a pause of goodwill', six weeks to change his mind.

It was a tense time, full of conflicting signals. While Saddam agreed to release all the Western hostages in early December, he prevaricated over the date for talks between his foreign minister, Tariq Aziz, and James Baker, the US secretary of state. It was still unclear whether he wanted a deal, or thought he could win a war. And behind the late talk of peace, the drums of war were sounding throughout the West. The Ministry of Defence in London asked for volunteer medical reservists, and when not enough came forward, initiated legislation not seen since the Korean war to call them up. The Prince of Wales visited the troops, and was followed in the New Year by John Major, the new prime minister, who had replaced Mrs Thatcher in a leadership election on November 28. The realists, especially the generals, knew war was coming. They felt they would win, but they could not be sure. They knew the allies had the technology and training, but they faced an enemy who had fought hard before. They also believed that it would almost certainly end in the trenches, with fixed bayonets. It was a sobering thought over Christmas and the New Year.

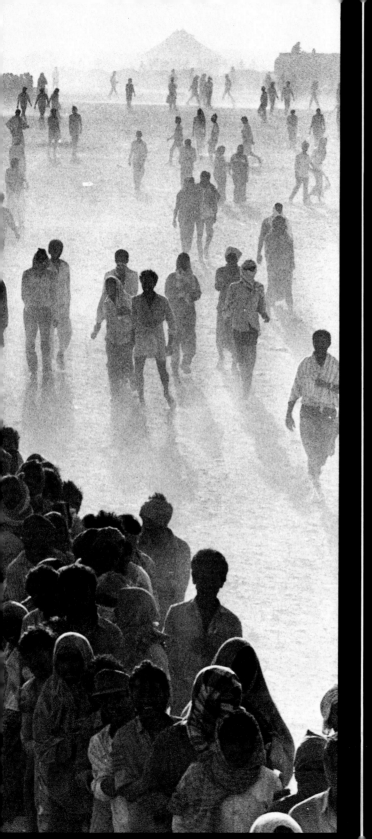

THE HUMAN COST

Previous pages: One of the queues at Sha'alan Two refugee camp near the Jordanian border. This was to be the scene of intense hardship as hundreds of thousands of expatriates, fearing war, sought to flee Iraq and Kuwait. Many were from Third World countries and had to wait here and at other camps for transport back to their own countries. Amid great heat and with inadequate sanitation, a growing number succumbed to illness (Simon Townsley/ *Sunday Times*)

Right: The camps were placed in arid desert where there was a desperate shortage of food and water. The crowd here is seen fighting to get bottled water after queueing for hours. Others were forced to buy drinks at extortionate prices from speculators. The shortages led to violence, with fights and robberies. Crown Prince Hassan described the camps as 'a human tragedy of the widest proportions' (Chip Hires–Gamma/FSP)

SADDAM'S invasion of Kuwait did more than occupy a country and terrorise its people; it scattered its huge expatriate population across the deserts. Suddenly hundreds of thousands of people were swilling around the region in search of a means of escape. Many of them came from poorer Arab countries and the Third World, and their harsh fate was to sit sweltering in the refugee camps along the Iraqi-Jordanian border, or to tramp north to Turkey and east to Iran. It was suffering on a massive scale, and several were to perish before they finally made their way home.

The rush to escape from Kuwait began within hours of the invasion. First were the thousands of Kuwaitis fleeing into Saudi Arabia, where they could be found sleeping in their BMWs and Mercedes at the border. Some Westerners also fled south, bringing the first tales of pillage and mayhem. For most expatriates, however, that route was closed, so cavalcades of Egyptians, Pakistanis, Filipinos and Bangladeshis headed north. There they were joined by the hundreds of thousands who worked in Iraq, equally eager to leave the likely crucible of war. This was altogether a different diaspora from the one in Saudi Arabia. Most were poor, working for a pittance at menial jobs for their Arab masters. In all an estimated three million expatriates had been working in both countries before August 2. More than a third of them were to escape by one means or another.

For most it was a traumatic journey accompanied at best by discomfort and at worst by tragedy. One group of Filipinos described how a young waitress had died on the road to Baghdad from apparent heat exhaustion. Many had already been forced to abandon their precious belongings in Kuwait, acquired after years of graft. Even if they managed to take their video recorders, cash and jewellery, they were frequently robbed on the way by avaricious Iraqi soldiers.

Transport was haphazard, and many had to pay exorbitant sums to get taken to the Jordanian border, where they were dumped in the desert with no food or water. There they found the frontier closed for long periods, so starting a wretched episode in the crisis. It did not take long for shanty camps to form, and for these to degenerate into places of suffering. The worst was called Sha'alan Two, which provided a form of temporary refuge to at least 60,000 of the detritus of the Third World. Though most were poor, the camps made little distinction. Professionals, who had given up a life of comfort in Kuwait, were forced to scrabble like dogs in the desert. Filipino maids, Bangladeshi drivers, Egyptian labourers, Indian bank clerks and Pakistani shopkeepers all huddled together, waiting. In one camp there were 80 Gurkhas who had been security guards. One wore his Falklands campaign T-shirt. Most pathetic of

all were the mothers with their children, wide-eyed and helpless.

Conditions were appalling. Endless queues snaked across the desert, thousands waiting for hours in temperatures of more than 40 degrees Celsius for water and a pot of yoghurt. Pathetic shelters of old cloth and luggage were erected to protect families from the sun and the merciless wind. At night, the temperature dropped sharply, and they huddled together for warmth. A *Sunday Times* journalist described it as a 'scene that could have come from a Mad Max film set in the aftermath of holocaust.' Inevitably, law and order began to break down. One Sri Lankan recalled how he had been attacked and beaten by two Pakistanis trying to steal his water. 'We are becoming savages here,' he said. Jordanian police waded in with truncheons and rubber hoses to restore order, but it was a half-hearted effort. Others fell prey to speculative traders, who prowled the fringes of the camps selling food and water at inflated prices. Equally inevitably, many began to suffer from dehydration, heat exhaustion, sunstroke and diarrhoea. Children began to die.

It was, in the words of Crown Prince Hassan of Jordan, 'a human tragedy of the widest proportions' for these 'downtrodden of the earth.' Amid this squalor, aid workers tried desperately to alleviate the suffering. *Médecins Sans Frontières* established some semblance of order in another camp, Sha'alan One. Gradually, the refugees were moved on to Jordan, where they waited with the quiet resignation of the dispossessed for flights home. Egyptians headed for the port of Aqaba and thence by boat across the Red Sea. Palestinians joined their people in Jordan or crossed the Allenby bridge into an equally uncertain fate in the Occupied West Bank. By the second week after the invasion, 50,000 were thought to have entered Jordan. By early October, there were 170,000 Indians trapped in Jordan, awaiting, as one Indian diplomat said, 'the biggest airlift since the Second World War.'

Meanwhile, 12,000 Westerners were still in Iraq and Kuwait – including about 2,500 Britons in Kuwait City. Most had gone into hiding, where they debated whether to try to escape across the desert or hold out. It soon occurred to Saddam – conscious of the United States'

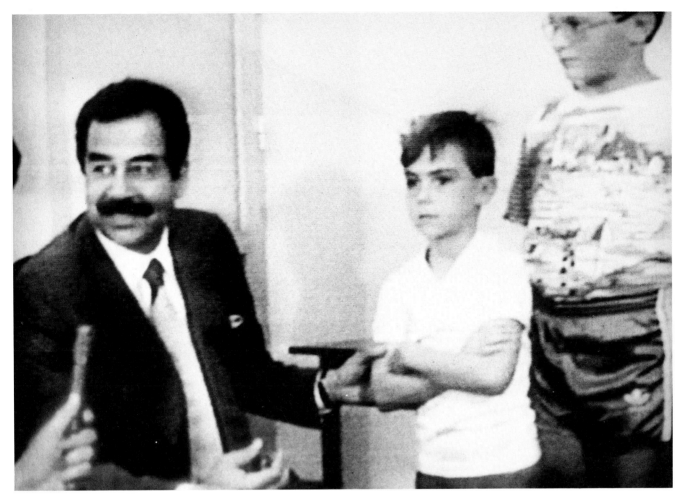

Left: The West was filled with revulsion when Saddam Hussein met British hostages in his first appearance on television after the invasion of Kuwait. He told the worried group, many of them women and children, that they were not hostages and that they were playing a valuable role in deterring war. Among them was a small boy, Stuart Lockwood, who was used as a prop by Saddam to show his concern over their well-being. It was not a convincing performance

humiliation by Iran during an earlier hostage crisis – that he had a ready-made bargaining chip. The expatriates could be used to deter an attack simply by holding them, or better still, placing them at likely targets for allied bombers, forming in effect a human shield. This started a long and painful game of cat and mouse with the lives of thousands of people.

Soon after the invasion a number of Westerners fled south to Saudi Arabia, braving Iraqi patrols and aided by Bedouin guides. One Briton, Douglas Croskery, was shot dead by Iraqis after he had stopped to help a group of fleeing Kuwaitis, but most made the tense journey without mishap. Others, for a variety of reasons, chose to stay and those not in hiding were gradually rounded up by Iraqi troops.

Among them was a group of British military advisers and the 337 passengers who were trapped on board flight BA149. It was obvious what the Iraqis had in mind, but for some time both London and Washington refused to use the 'h' word for fear of reviving memories of the Carter fiasco. The Iraqis too, played the game. Tariq Aziz, the foreign minister, became a master

of this curious ritual. The hostages, he said, 'were not hostages. We would like to keep them as guests for a while to live with our people.' Saddam said they were there to save the lives of other foreigners.The Iraqis even started a television programme called 'Guest News', when hostages could send messages home. The manipulation was invariably unsubtle. They invited wives of hostages from Britain for Christmas in Baghdad, and arranged an elaborate wedding for a couple in front of the television cameras.

But the incident which had the greatest impact on Western public opinion was Saddam's first appearance after the invasion, when he decided to visit some of his British guests. He wanted to explain to them that they were not hostages and that they they were playing a valuable role in deterring war. The argument, and his false concern for their well-being, prompted a sense of revulsion, which was heightened when he suggested a group photograph. Among the guests was a small boy, Stuart Lockwood, whose tense, pale face stared out from the television screens as Saddam stroked his head. The six-year-old boy, shrinking instinctively from the

Right: Jesse Jackson, the Democratic former presidential candidate and now a television personality, was one of the first of a welter of statesmen to visit Saddam to plead for the release of the hostages. Saddam took him to Kuwait City and then allowed him to leave with a group of American and British hostages, including the British boy, Stuart Lockwood (Rex Features)

Centre right: A family are reunited at Houston airport. At the outset of the crisis, there were about 12,000 Westerners in Iraq and Kuwait, and Saddam sought to use concern over their safety to drive wedges between the coalition forming against him. Some nationalities were released if their governments appeared less hostile to Iraq (Gamma/FSP)

Left: Kurt Waldheim, the Austrian president, was the first to lead the rush among elder Western statesmen. He is seen here being greeted by Saddam Hussein in Baghdad. He, too, was allowed to take home a group of 95 Austrians (Kurz–Gamma/FSP)j

Below: Edward Heath, the former Conservative prime minister, was a vocal critic of the West in its confrontation with Saddam. Despite criticism at home, he visited Baghdad and met Saddam on October 21. He was allowed to bring out a group of sick British citizens and is seen here celebrating with freed hostages on a Virgin flight to Gatwick from Baghdad (Press Association)

touch of the Iraqi president, was meant as a prop to display Saddam's generous nature and affection for children. He achieved quite the reverse.

By now Bush had accepted that he was dealing with a hostage crisis and began to refer to the Westerners as 'pawns'. At first Saddam played the game well, exploiting weaknesses and rivalries. After a while women and children were allowed out, while the men had to stay. Some nationalities – such as the French and Germans – were released, while others were not. And as he freed some, he detained others. To him it was a means of maintaining political pressure without dramatically escalating the crisis.

The Americans viewed developments with growing alarm, although Bush was determined not to be seen to be preoccupied with their plight. At one time the crisis was thought to have been accelerating the logic of war. But the military was reluctant to move until it was ready, and Bush limited himself to making angry statements. In mid-November, he said that he had 'had it with that kind of treatment of Americans,' while Mrs Thatcher taunted Saddam by accusing him of hiding behind the skirts of women. For the hostages it was a frightening

period, being shunted from place to place and not knowing whether they were to be punished or not. Many wives had to leave their husbands behind. Some Iraqis showed considerable friendliness and humanity. But there were cases of maltreatment and bullying.

All suffered some form of privation, the luckier ones little more than boredom. 'Conditions can't be described as comfortable,' said one hostage with considerable understatement. One man said his group had rioted because of their treatment by sadistic guards and a starvation diet of rice and bread. Others underwent considerable discomfort on long bus rides in great heat with no water or air conditioning. And while some stayed in squalid tin huts, others were held at the Kuwaiti Regency Palace, one of the world's 200 most luxurious hotels, where they enjoyed the indoor tennis courts and delicacies produced by a French chef.

Quite a few were soon bussed to strategic sites, including factories and airfields. But instead of weakening the West's will to fight, Saddam merely succeeded in enraging people. American public opinion, at first wary of war, was fully behind military retaliation if any of the hostages were harmed. Even Saddam's few

friends – such as Yasser Arafat, leader of the Palestine Liberation Organisation, and King Hussein of Jordan – advised him to free them.

For months the drama preoccupied the West, and as war drew closer it seemed that Saddam was prepared to sacrifice the hostages. But gradually the arguments began to have effect and he became convinced that they were causing him more trouble than they were worth. He then tried one last gambit. At the end of November he promised to release all hostages by March 25 as long as there was no allied attack. By then three quarters of the Westerners had fled or been released. Only about 1,200 Britons, 700 Americans and scores from other nationalities were left. An estimated 600 were being held at strategic sites.

The West refused to make any such bargain, and Saddam had to relent. On December 6, he ordered the release of all foreigners 'with our apologies for any harm'. Many in the Arab world wrongly took it to mean that he was seeking a face-saving way out and was about to bargain a withdrawal. In reality it was a decision he was later said to have regretted. Bush certainly saw it differently. It was a step, he said, that 'cleared the decks' for action.

With a UN deadline of January 15 fast approaching, a mood of allied determination was replacing the vacillation of the autumn. By the end of November Bush seemed set on a military solution, and during a trip to Europe and Saudi Arabia – when he spent Thanksgiving with US troops in the desert – he sounded increasingly impatient. But however hopeless the situation, he knew he had to make one last effort to avoid war. In early December, he offered 'to go that extra mile for peace' and invited Tariq Aziz to Washington and suggested that James Baker, the secretary of state, should go to Baghdad to confront Saddam with the unappetising realities. For Bush the crisis had entered a dangerous phase, with intense debate in Congress about Gulf policy and America's role in the world. The public, while supporting him, also showed a reluctance to fight. It was not the mood of Britain, where John Major had overwhelming support for military action. Bush was facing the same isolationist tendencies that confronted Woodrow Wilson during the First World War and Franklin Roosevelt in the second.

Once again Saddam was to seal his own fate. He shunned Algerian peace efforts and vacillated over a date for Baker to visit Baghdad. William Webster, head of the CIA, came to the conclusion that Saddam thought he could stall 'until the first shell is lobbed over him.' When Baker and Aziz met in Geneva on January 9, the talks broke down after six hours. The way was now open for war.

THE
BOMBING
OF
BAGHDAD

Previous pages: The night sky over Baghdad erupts with Iraqi anti-aircraft fire at 2.32am on January 17 as allied bombers begin the biggest raid since the Second World War. One witness said it looked like a 'million fireflies'. Despite the impressive display, most of the ground fire was undirected and failed to hit any aircraft. The Stealth F-117s – invisible to Iraqi radar – led the attack using precision-guided 'smart' bombs. Within the first few hours they hit key command and control targets and struck communications centres, causing almost no damage to surrounding buildings. At the same time Tomahawk cruise missiles were slamming into buildings. The F-117s and other bombers were to return to Baghdad and its outskirts almost every night of the war, demolishing air defences, power stations, military headquarters and communications (Dominique Mollard/AP)

Right: The result of a raid in Baghdad using a 2,000 pound precision-guided bomb (Noel Quidu– Gamma/FSP)

JUST before midnight of January 16, John Major sat alone in his flat upstairs at 10 Downing Street watching television. He had a speech to prepare, but it lay beside him unattended as he gazed at the screen. Flickering in front of him was the night sky over Baghdad, dissected by tracers and missiles soaring into the heavens. The effect was of a violent electrical storm. To a background din of rolling crashes, the breathless voices of John Holliman, Peter Arnett and Bernard Shaw, the CNN television team in Baghdad, announced the start of the biggest air raid since the Second World War.

For 24 hours, the prime minister had been one of only five people in Britain who knew that the air blitz was about to begin. Now the whole world knew, thanks to the TV and radio reporters poking their cameras and microphones out of the windows of the al-Rashid hotel. Major stayed awake all night watching the bombing in lonely fascination. Occasionally his foreign policy adviser, Sir Charles Powell, would pop in with news from the Gulf or Washington, where George Bush also sat absorbed in front of CNN, flicking occasionally to the other networks. Like almost everyone else, Bush had come to rely on television for war coverage; he even carried a portable set with him when he went on walks.

He had taken the decision to go to war about thirty hours earlier, and now seemed less fidgety than he had been for the previous few days. Everything seemed to be going according to plan. At 6.37pm Washington time, ABC interrupted its news broadcast with a dramatic live telephone call from Gary Shepard, the network's correspondent in Baghdad. 'Throughout the entire sky there are flashes of light. Something is definitely under way here.' Bush said quietly, 'Just the way it was scheduled.' Twenty minutes later, Marlin Fitzwater, the unassuming White House spokesman, was sent to tell reporters that 'the liberation of Kuwait has begun.' It was five months and fifteen days since Saddam Hussein had invaded.

In Riyadh, Lieutenant General Charles 'Chuck' Horner and Brigadier General Buster Glosson were in the TACC, known to outsiders as the Black Hole, an underground bunker from where they were directing the blitzkrieg on Baghdad. Despite all their paraphernalia of war, with huge radar screens full of blips showing where the air armada was heading, they wanted some real, live intelligence. Horner sent an aide upstairs to watch CNN. 'What are they saying?' he demanded on the telephone. 'Bernie Shaw's under the table,' said the aide. Horner checked his watch. The telephone exchange – needed by CNN to transmit its pictures – was due to be hit at just about that moment. There was

a huge explosion. 'What's Bernie Shaw saying now?' asked Horner. 'He just went off the air,' replied the aide.

The timing of the start of the air war was inevitably a closely-guarded secret. Only the leaders of the main alliance powers had been told of American plans. Bush had spoken for forty-five minutes on the telephone with Major. Both men agreed, as one aide put it, that 'we've tried for peace and it hasn't worked. He's chosen for war, so let's do it.' Major then told the Queen, Tom King, the defence minister, and Douglas Hurd, the foreign secretary. Neil Kinnock, leader of the opposition, was not informed. Bush had also called Mikhail Gorbachev, who had appealed for more time for diplomacy.

In Washington, among the first to hear of the plans on Wednesday morning was Prince Bandar bin Sultan, the highly-regarded Saudi ambassador. James Baker called him to the state department and told him: 'Bandar, the balloon is about to go up. This is your notification.' It was just what the Saudi royal family had wanted to hear. The prince, a favourite nephew of King Fahd and a former fighter pilot, went into an adjoining room and telephoned his uncle in Riyadh. In accordance with an agreed plan, Bandar used a password which indicated the United States was formally requesting permission to attack. The king replied with another password giving his assent.

What followed that night over Baghdad was the result of the most intricate planning, an elegant choreography of destruction. Computers had been

Left: Crewmen from the USS *Wisconsin* watch as a Tomahawk cruise missile is fired towards Baghdad in the first days of the air war. The missile climbs to an altitude of several hundred feet before dropping down to hug the contours of the land as it follows a pre-programmed flight path. Almost all hit their targets (John McCutcheon/San Diego Union)

Above: A cruise missile on the final leg of its mission is photographed flying at 500mph over treetops in Baghdad (Sipa/Rex)

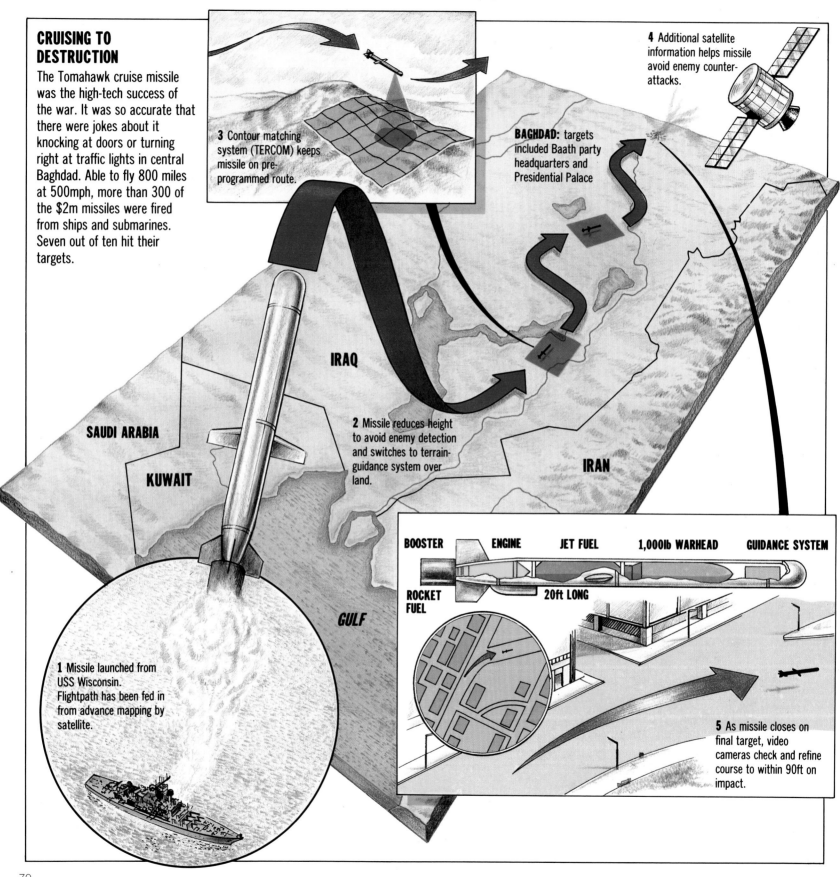

CRUISING TO DESTRUCTION

The Tomahawk cruise missile was the high-tech success of the war. It was so accurate that there were jokes about it knocking at doors or turning right at traffic lights in central Baghdad. Able to fly 800 miles at 500mph, more than 300 of the $2m missiles were fired from ships and submarines. Seven out of ten hit their targets.

3 Contour matching system (TERCOM) keeps missile on pre-programmed route.

4 Additional satellite information helps missile avoid enemy counter-attacks.

BAGHDAD: targets included Baath party headquarters and Presidential Palace

IRAQ

SAUDI ARABIA

KUWAIT

IRAN

2 Missile reduces height to avoid enemy detection and switches to terrain-guidance system over land.

GULF

1 Missile launched from USS Wisconsin. Flightpath has been fed in from advance mapping by satellite.

BOOSTER **ENGINE** **JET FUEL** **1,000lb WARHEAD** **GUIDANCE SYSTEM**

ROCKET FUEL

20ft LONG

5 As missile closes on final target, video cameras check and refine course to within 90ft on impact.

The scarlet tracery of anti-aircraft fire lights the sky over Baghdad on the night of January 17 during the allies' first bombing raid on the city (Laurent van der Stockt–Gamma/FSP)

Anti-aircraft guns fire from a rooftop in Baghdad on January 17, the first day of the five-week air campaign. After Iraq invaded Kuwait on August 2, the city had been steadily building its air defences, placing the guns by helicopter on flat roofs. It was a largely pointless exercise; no allied aricraft were shot down over Baghdad. Most of the time the Iraqis could not even see what they were firing at. They did, however, succeed in shooting down cruise missiles, at some risk to civilians (Andy Hernandez –Sipa/Rex)

churning away for months to find a means of heaping as much high explosive on the city as possible with minimal losses for allied aircraft and the civilian population. Pride of place went to the Stealth F-117 fighter-bombers, the almost undetectable bat-like aircraft which could lob laser-guided bombs with breathtaking precision. Their pilots call them 'wobbly goblins' and the Saudis 'shabahs', or 'ghosts'. At almost the same time as they began their raids – it was deliberately not simultaneous – Tomahawk cruise missiles fired from warships and submarines in the Gulf and Red Sea slammed into command and control targets, including the Presidential Palace and the Ministry of Defence. Overhead, US Navy EA-6 Prowlers and the USAF EF-111S Ravens jammed Iraqi radar systems, blinding the Iraqis electronically. Behind them came the Wild Weasels, the F-4Gs, whose HARM rockets destroyed radar-guided surface-to-air missiles. Everything was timed to the nearest second to clear the way for the bombers. Controlling it all from the air were the AWACS, the giant aircraft with radar mushrooms that could 'see' for hundreds of miles.

The raid seemed to catch the Iraqis off guard. No one had thought to switch off the city's lights. The four minarets and golden dome of the Kadhimiya mosque were lit up to remind citizens of Baghdad's glorious past and Saddam's new-found religious zeal. It took some minutes before the army realised the war had started; then they began to fire the 'Triple A' – the anti-aircraft artillery. Captain Steve Tate, who was flying an F-15 over Baghdad, said it reminded him of a 'huge blanket of Christmas lights. The entire city was just sparkling at us, shooting 'Triple A'.'

Pilots struggled to find words to describe the view from their cockpits. For Colonel George Walton, flying a F-4G Wild Weasel, it was 'one of the most fantastic firework demonstrations ever, just like the Fourth of July.' Another said it was 'just like the movies, like Apocalypse Now.' The anti-aircraft fire was intense. Horner said it was 'in some areas the most difficult assembled anywhere in the world.' Tate was to contribute to the pyrotechnics by being the first allied pilot to shoot down an enemy plane, a rare feat given Iraqi reluctance to engage in combat. Flying above 'a package of bombers', he detected a radar contact moving rapidly towards the tail of one of his flight of four F-15s. 'I locked him up,' said Tate, 'confirmed he was hostile and fired a missile. When the airplane blew up, the whole sky lit up. It burned all the way to the ground and then blew up into a thousand pieces.'

Once the war started and seemed to be going well, there was relief throughout the West and among Arab allies. Iraq was such an unknown quantity, with so much

A man surveys the
damage in Baghdad of an
allied bombing raid which
hit a group of houses
(Noel Quidu-Gamma/FSP)

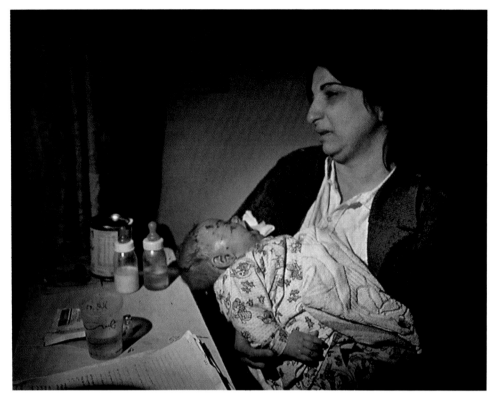

military hardware, that almost anything could have happened. Many, too, had doubts about the Americans, engendered by failed missions and the Vietnam war. It was almost as if they believed the same myths as Saddam Hussein, who had vowed to given them another Vietnam in the sand. So far, Desert Storm was almost faultless. Stock markets soared and oil prices fell. After his long night vigil, a smiling John Major appeared in front of Downing Street following a 7am war cabinet meeting. At the Pentagon, officials spoke of having 'decimated' the Iraqi air force and claimed they had severely damaged chemical and nuclear facilities and harmed Saddam's command and control system. The upbeat mood continued when Richard Cheney, the defence secretary, and Baker arrived at the White House for breakfast. Cheney was carrying satellite pictures which showed how cruise missiles had hit Saddam's palace and defence ministry. It was a happy party which left for a religious service organised by Billy Graham, the evangelical leader and friend of Bush, at a base in Fort Myers, Virginia.

The people of Baghdad, however, were feeling far from happy. A sense of unease had gripped the city as the January15 deadline had passed. Many had already left, or sent their families away. They expected bombing, but were gripped by a strange fatalism; foreign radio broadcasts had led them to believe the city might

An Iraqi mother weeps as she nurses her wounded baby. Despite allied attempts to use precision-guided weapons to keep civilian casualties to a minimum, an undisclosed number of Iraqis were killed and injured in raids on Baghdad (Ali Yurtsever–Gamma/FSP)

Above: Smoke rises from a bombing raid behind a statue of Saddam Hussein (Ali Yurtsever– Gamma/ FSP)

Left: The building which the Iraqis said was a baby milk plant and which the allies claimed was being used to make biological weapons (Ali Yurtsever– Gamma/FSP)

Far left: Two British Jaguar jet fighters take off on their bombing mission over Iraq (David Giles– AFP/Popperfoto)

Video shots taken by French Jaguar pilots as they destroyed a bridge over the Tigris. Film displays of 'smart' missiles and bombs hitting targets were to become a high-tech feature of the war (Gilles Bassignac–Gamma/ FSP)

Far right: The same bridge as shown on the video. Bridges were a prime target for allied bombers, the main aim being to cut supplies to the army in the south and generally destroy the infrastructure. On January 30 General Norman Schwarzkopf said that US planes had flown no less than 790 sorties against 33 bridges. On February 9, it was estimated that half of these bridges had been destroyed. By the start of the land war, almost all were out of operation (Ali Yurtsever–Gamma/FSP)

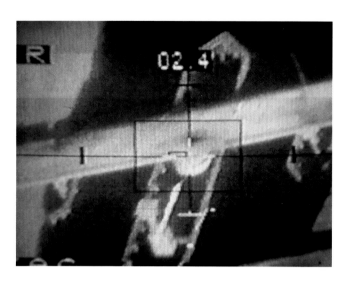

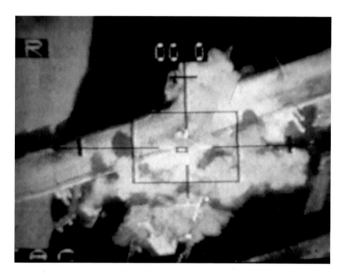

be flattened. Nothing they had experienced during the Iran–Iraq war, however, had prepared them for the onslaught which began at 2.32am on January 17. No Arab city had ever experienced so much devastation in so short a time.

That night, on the fifth floor of the al-Rashid hotel, reporters watched the tracer fire and missiles spewing across the sky. They described how white flashes illuminated the tops of buildings where aircraft batteries had sat patiently for months. Now they pumped their shells into the sky without even seeing their enemies. Strange video game noises filled the air. The impact of bombs buffeted the building. Below, in the hotel's bomb shelter, women chanted 'Palestine! Palestine!'

The morning dawned cold and misty. Smoke hung over the city, but there seemed little sign of the damage. Baghdad radio was in defiant mood: 'This is communique number one. The mother of battles has begun. President Bush will regret this attack. Victory is near.'

For those venturing out, the first evidence of bombing was at the city's tele-communications building. It had been hit by at least four laser-guided bombs delivered by Stealth aircraft. Though chunks of concrete littered the streets, some neighbouring buildings had little more than broken windows.

It was the first sign of the technological prowess of American weapons. The cruise missiles had found their targets with great accuracy. Journalists saw them whizzing over their heads or flying past hotel windows, almost as if they were following street signs. The Baath party headquarters had been hit, as had the Presidential Palace. That morning the defence ministry, an old Ottoman building that was still marked as the Abbassid Palace on tourist maps, was struck again by a cruise. There was nobody inside; the Iraqis had evacuated the building. Bombs also hit gas and oil storage plants on the outskirts and army barracks.

The people of Baghdad, renowned for their *sang froid*, affected an air of unconcern as the bombs rained down. There was little sign of panic. Some stood in the streets with luggage, apparently waiting to leave. Others formed orderly queues for bread and petrol. Militiamen, often teenagers in jeans and carrying Kalashnikovs, appeared to keep order. But there was no need. The city was in a state of shock. Saddam broadcast on the radio at 12.40pm. It was vintage rhetoric, even by his standards. 'At 2.30am the great duel started. The valiant sons of Iraq, your brothers, sons and fathers, confronted the invaders. Damn King Fahd, the traitor of Mecca, damn the invaders, damn these criminals. We shall win. The dawn will break and they will be damned.'

Some residents expressed surprise that the bombing had not been more devastating. Their mood was defiant; 'if that was it, we can take it,' said one resident. Others were confused. 'We never thought it would come to this,' a merchant said. 'It's madness, madness. Kuwait isn't worth this – not to us, not to you.' But it was only the beginning. For the next forty days and forty nights the city was to be relentlessly pounded. And gradually the air raids began to take their toll, demolishing key installations and services. Electricity and telephones were cut. Shops stayed closed; those that didn't charged exorbitant prices, still selling some of the looted goods from Kuwait. Water supplies dried up and the streets filled with sewage and rubbish. Bridges across the Tigris were bombed. Those Baghdadis that hadn't fled began to leave. Iraq tried to undermine the allied portrayal of the assault as a triumph of the 'smart bomb'. At the end of January the Baghdad government accused the Americans of bombing a 'baby milk factory'. The allies maintained it was a plant for making biological weapons.

On February 13 at 4am, two Stealth F-117 bombers struck at what the allies believed was an important command and control bunker. It turned out to be packed with civilians, many of them women and children. A total of 314 people died as a 2,000 pound laser-guided bomb with a delayed fuse entered a ventilation shaft and exploded on an upper floor. It was the worst moment of the Gulf war, when the video fantasies of briefing sessions gave way to charred flesh. The raid was the single biggest loss of civilian life in the war and sent a shock through the alliance. The Iraqis claimed the Amiriya building was used solely as a shelter, and reporters in Baghdad found no evidence of military hardware or a secret subterranean level. But the allies said they had evidence which could not be revealed and stuck by their story. In private they admitted they had made a mistake by not finding out in advance that civilians were in the shelter. The raid was to lead to greater interference by the Joint Chiefs of Staff over the choice of targets.

Right: Distressed relatives discover they have lost members of their family in the shelter

Centre right: Rescue workers collect the charred remains from the shelter (Dilip Ganguly/AP)

Bottom right: A boy wounded in the bunker raid is filmed by French television

The bombing of Baghdad continued with varying intensity for the next month. On some nights it was hit hard, on others left almost alone. On February 19, just before Saddam was to receive details of a Soviet peace plan, the city experienced some of the heaviest bombing of the war. An Egyptian who fled described what it was like for the unprivileged who had nowhere to hide: 'When the sirens scream the people run to the shelters, but the shelters are full. If you can't get in, you curl up near the entrance for comfort. And the next day you hear "so and so's family is dead".' Another spoke of the terror of running down streets at night and the irrational fear of being hit by an anti-aircraft shell falling back to earth.

In the Black Hole in Riyadh, they had prepared a long targetting list for Baghdad and were gradually working though it. Some wanted to include the al-Rashid hotel,

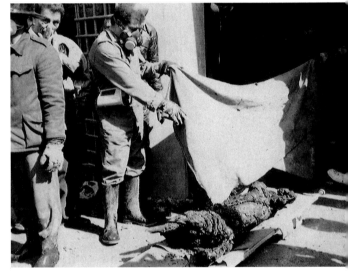

whose underground bomb shelter apparently hid a command and control unit. That was ruled out because of journalists and foreigners staying in the building. There was also debate about including such non-military targets as the Baath Party headquarters; it was included because it was an integral part of Saddam's regime and destroying it would help undermine morale. That, too, was the argument for hitting services, such as electricity and water. The high command in Riyadh wanted to take the war to Saddam's front door.

That was before the Amiriya bombing. On February 13 at 4am, two F-117 Stealths – the aircraft responsible for ninety-five per cent of the damage inflicted on Baghdad – dropped two laser-guided bombs on to a building in a wealthy suburb. The allies had pinpointed it as an important command and control bunker, sending

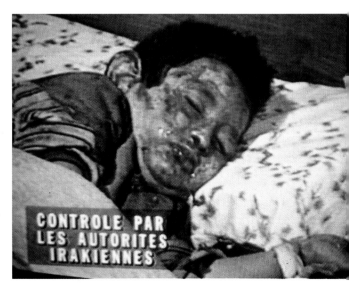

CONTROLE PAR LES AUTORITES IRAKIENNES

Smoke escaping from the shelter hours after the raid

messages to the front. It was also one of a dozen or so bunkers designed to shelter the ruling elite, families of the small inner circle of Takritis who controlled the country. The rest of the population had to seek shelter where they could find it. But inside Amiriya were hundreds of women and children who had routinely hidden there ever since the raids had started.

At one level the allies had done their work carefully, obtaining the plans for the bunker from the Scandinavian contractors who helped build it and monitoring its use by satellites and surveillance aircraft. They had intended to place both 2,000 pound bombs down ventilation shafts, but one missed and exploded near the entrance, blocking the only escape route. The other was on target, plunging into the bunker and exploding in the middle of the largest room on the upper floor. The effect

was horrendous; 314 people died, about 130 of them children. The scenes of badly-burned bodies being hauled out and distraught relatives gathering outside shook the international alliance and brought home the human cost of a war that until then had seemed as remote as a high-tech video game. The Iraqis were quick to exploit the propaganda value of the bombing by allowing Western television for the first time to report an event uncensored.

The scenes were harrowing. Filmed in hospital, Onar Adnan, aged seventeen, explained that he had lost his parents and three sisters. 'I was sleeping and suddenly I felt heat and the blanket was burning,' he said. 'I turned to try and touch my mother who was next to me, but I grabbed nothing but a piece of flesh.' A man who had lost his family of twelve screamed at Western

Bodies placed in the back of a coach before being taken to the morgue. The bombing created many personal tragedies. One wounded boy lost his entire family. A lawyer had taken his wife, two daughters and his son to the shelter but had gone home. When he returned soon after the bombing, he discovered they had all been killed. (J.M.Bourget/ Paris Match)

journalists. 'My God! My God! All of them are dead. Why? Why are you killing all the Iraqi children?'

It was a question that flashed between Riyadh and Washington; why had they not been told there were women and children inside the building? As the first CNN reports reached Centcom, many senior officers assumed they had hit the wrong target. General Norman Schwarzkopf was said to be 'concerned, perplexed and generally damned upset.' He knew the damage it could do to the alliance and the interference it might encourage from Washington. He demanded an explanation, 'fast'.

Despite reporters in Baghdad finding no evidence that the shelter had been used for military purposes, Schwarzkopf's commanders gave him signals intelligence that showed the bunker had been used to transmit messages. There were other indications; military vehicles occasionally outside, visits by Saddam, a camouflaged roof. Some commanders speculated that they had been 'set up' by the Iraqi president and that he had deliberately placed civilians inside to score a propaganda victory. That seemed unlikely, but the evidence of military use was enough to satisfy 'the Bear' and his political masters. In public, at any rate, the Pentagon and Bush defended the bombing of a legitimate military target. In private, however, the story was different. One Pentagon official admitted it was a mistake: 'The satellite reconnaissance said this was a deep, multi-faceted bunker. But there was very little on the ground assessment and we had no idea civilians were there,' he said.

Part of the explanation for the bombing may have been the Americans' unstated determination 'to decapitate' the leadership. While they might not kill Saddam, they could weaken his authority and possibly encourage his overthrow. They might well have assumed there would be members of the leadership in the bunker. Several recalled the words of General Michael Dugan, the US air force chief of staff, who was fired by Cheney at the end of 1990 for saying publicly that 'the cutting edge would be in downtown Baghdad'.

Military target or not, a raid on the bunker could have done considerable harm to the small group around Saddam. The fact that it killed many privileged women and children was an unfortunate mistake. After the bombing, the politicians in Washington demanded more say in what was to be attacked. Colin Powell, chairman of the Joint Chiefs of Staff, now studied all targets. The air forces' remarkable freedom to bomb whatever they liked had been eroded. But by then the air war was all but won.

SCUD
WARS

I T BEGAN with an eerie, blood-chilling wail of the air raid sirens at 2am, almost exactly twenty-four hours after the first planes had screamed over Baghdad. Across Israel people scrambled from their beds, grabbed gas masks and syringes of atropine against nerve agents, and ran to specially-prepared rooms sealed with masking tape. They had been told there would be plenty of warning of missile attacks, but the first crump of an exploding warhead came almost immediately. Aby Itzchaki was on the streets of Tel Aviv, rushing home as the sirens shrieked, when he saw what he described as a 'shooting star with a red nose' flash over the city. The sky suddenly lit up and and buildings shook to a deafening blast. Against all the odds, Saddam Hussein had scored his first direct hit on an Israeli city. More missiles followed, two hitting Tel Aviv and two the port of Haifa. Others fell off target.

The next hour was to be etched on the memories of three million Jews, all too conscious of their history as victims of gas. They had been expecting to be hit – the people of Tel Aviv joked that they were Saddam's number one target and as a result almost certainly safe. But it was only a joke, and when the missiles came it did not lessen the shock and surprise. Saddam had promised to incinerate 'the Zionist entity', and despite forty years of almost constant conflict, Israel had never before come under ballistic missile attack and certainly had never been threatened with poison gas. Now, within eight minutes, eight Scuds streaked across the sky.

The first blast in Tel Aviv wrecked a dozen or more houses in a working-class district and shattered

windows up to a mile away. Miraculously, only twelve people were injured by the explosions, but they were not the only victims. A three-year-old child died as her parents tried to get her gas mask on. And three elderly women, alone and confused, suffocated because they were unable to remove a cap on the filter of the masks.

The police and army were instantly convinced it was a nerve gas attack. One report said that gas victims were being taken to hospital. Locked away in their sealed rooms, the people of Israel knew no better. Their only contact with the outside world was the radio, which blasted out cheerful tunes in between news bulletins. Outside, there was the incessant roar of jet engines as Israeli warplanes scrambled to meet any air attack. A few panicked, and injected themselves with the atropine. The antidote caused some of the symptons of poisoning, further heightening the panic.

After about an hour, people were told in English, Hebrew, Russian and Arabic that they could take off their masks. Gas had not been used. It was a relief; but it was only the start of a long and tense period. No one was sure whether Saddam had the capability to adapt his Scud missiles to carry poison gas. It required a sophisticated means of releasing clouds of gas above a city as the missile hurtled to earth. That may only have been the practice run, they said. The Germans had helped Saddam modify his Scuds, and they had also helped him manufacture his poison gas. Who was to say the next volley would not spread sarin or other ghastly poisons over the rooftops?

That weekend Tel Aviv began to empty. Vehicles streamed out of the city, past the craters and levelled houses, heading for Tiberias, on the Sea of Galilee, or Jerusalem, or any likely refuge. There was no obvious panic, though some politicians began to adopt the apocalyptic language of the Bible: 'This is a war of the Children of Light against the Children of Darkness,' pronounced David Levy, the foreign minister.

The rest of the world was more interested in whether the Children of Light would retaliate. Iraq's intention was obvious, but no less threatening for that. The possible involvement of Israel had been a constant worry to the allies ever since the crisis began. If Israel entered the war on the side of the coalition, how would Syria, Egypt and Saudi Arabia react? And even if their governments held firm, there was no guarantee they could carry the people, who had been raised to detest Israel. The allies worried that Israel might fire its own Jericho missiles at Baghdad, or worse, use nuclear weapons if it came under gas attack. Many in the West regarded the Israelis as unpredictable, willing to do almost anything to defend their right to retaliate. A long history of persecution had taught them not to rely on others.

Far left: A Palestinian woman in the West Bank telling foreign journalists that a missile which hit a neighbouring village was an American Patriot, not a Scud. In fact Saddam's missiles occasionally fell short of Tel Aviv, landing in the West Bank. The Palestinians had a bad war, cheering whenever a Scud was fired at Israel but in fear of their own lives from a gas attack; the Israelis had limited the distribution of gas masks to prevent them being used by demonstrators for protection from police tear gas. Despite erratic Iraqi aim, Saddam remained a hero. Many named their children 'Saddam' or 'Scud' (Simon Townsley/ *Sunday Times*)

Left: Rescue workers return at first light to the Ramat Gan district of Tel Aviv to search for bodies amid wrecked houses. Twelve Israelis died – several from shock or problems with gas masks – and 305 were injured during the Scud wars. Only US diplomatic pressure and the offer of American-manned Patriot missiles prevented Israel from entering the war. It was a constant concern to the allies that Israel would ignore the calls for restraint and attack Scud sites or fire its own ballistic missiles at Baghdad. But Israel held back, winning international acclaim (Sally Soames/*Sunday Times*)

John Major was woken with news of the attacks at about 1am by the ever-present Charles Powell. They went into a well-rehearsed programme of damage control. The Israeli ambassador was called and urged to convey to his government Britain's desire for restraint. In Washington, the news had Richard Cheney, the defence secretary, on the telephone almost immediately to his opposite number, Moshe Arens. Arens professed to be furious and said Israel had scrambled a dozen aircraft and was about to attack Iraqi targets. He then issued an extraordinary list of demands; he wanted allied air codes which would prevent clashes with coalition forces. If they could not have those, Israel demanded a 'safe' corridor through which to attack, or a four-hour period when allied aircraft would hold off their raids. Arens claimed he was planning a combined air and ground assault and intended to put commandos into Iraq to attack Scud bases. As if that was not enough, he wanted the United States to use its influence with Jordan to allow them to pass through its airspace.

Cheney was horrified. He knew that if he agreed to any of those demands it would be catastrophic. He replied that Bush would never accept any such proposals. Confronted by American obduracy, Arens seemed to back off. But Washington could not be sure. James Baker, who had been walking out of the state department when he heard of the missile attacks, frantically worked the telephones, calling the ambassadors of Egypt, Syria and Saudi Arabia to warn them he might not be able to prevent an Israeli raid on Iraq.

Baker then hurried to the White House for a meeting of the war cabinet to debate how to keep Israel out of the war. One of those present said: 'We had felt we were doing so well, suddenly it was one of these nightmare scenarios.' George Bush, who had retired for dinner, called Yitzhak Shamir, the prime minister, to offer his condolences and to request Shamir not to respond. He offered him American-manned Patriot missiles, an air defence system designed to take out incoming missiles. Shamir had already refused these some weeks before, but with the reality of missiles falling out of the sky he now accepted the offer. Bush promised they would be operational almost immediately and within a day giant transporters were landing in Israel with the missiles on board.

They could not have come a moment too soon. Within twenty-four hours Israel was again under Scud attack. Injuries were restricted to sixteen, but retaliation again looked certain. One senior official said there would be something 'unexpected and spectacular'. Benjamin Netanyhu, the hawkish deputy foreign minister, who was becoming a star through regular television appearances, warned 'that it now becomes particularly understandable that Israel reserves the right to protect its citizens.' All this was enough to have Bush woken in the middle of the night at Camp David, where he was soon on the telephone again to Shamir appealing for restraint. This time Shamir told him they should leave the hunt for Scuds to the Israelis, allowing the allies more time to bomb strategic targets and troop concentrations. Shamir implied that at least the Israelis would be successful.

Bush demurred, and said he would step up the search. He did not tell Shamir that the allies had so far destroyed only ten mobile launchers. Publicly he was to promise 'the darndest search and destroy mission that's ever been undertaken.' Cheney had already told Arens that the hunt was being intensified and had promised to send special forces into western Iraq and to direct more aircraft to Scud-hunting. The Israelis could hardly complain; it was exactly what they had planned to do themselves.

The decision was to cause one of the few clashes of the war between the politicians and the military. Cheney complained the military was dragging its feet, while Norman Schwarzkopf, the allied commander, regarded the Scuds as no more than weapons of terror – flying petrol tanks with a grenade strapped to the end. If he started diverting more resources to their destruction, he argued, it would delay the air war and the land offensive. But the imperative of keeping Israel out of the war prevailed, and the hunt for Scuds was stepped up. It was not the end of the matter, though. Israel constantly kept the allies guessing, and at one stage even discussed raids into Iran to destroy the Iraqi planes which had fled there, or joint US–Israeli raids in which the Americans would provide air-to-air refuelling. These were politely discouraged. 'It was tense, very tense,' recalled one Pentagon official.

The man who had been sent in by Bush to try to defuse the crisis was Lawrence Eagleburger, an under secretary of state and a wily political operator. He had succeeded in his first aim of persuading the Israelis not to launch a pre-emptive strike against Iraq; now he had to use all his skill to persuade them not to retaliate. In this he was helped by a worldwide groundswell of sympathy for Israel, which increased the longer it showed restraint. For years it had been the butt of criticism for its harsh policy in the Occupied Territories; now it rather liked being hailed again as the plucky, beleaguered little state. Outsiders generously overlooked the fact that it had failed to provide gas masks to the Palestinians in the Occupied Territories. Eagleburger sought to persuade the Government it was in their interests to hold off and let the allies do the dirty work. He pointed out that Israeli involvement could jeopardise the alliance, perhaps allowing Saddam's military might to

An audience puts on gas masks during a Scud alert on February 23. The concert was given by Isaac Stern in Jerusalem. When the Israeli Philharmonic Orchestra left the stage, he fetched a violin and played a Mozart solo without his mask to an audience looking like a bunch of ants (Esaias Baitel/Gamma)

survive. That would only put off the threat to Israel to another day.

Eagleburger handled all this with skill and humour. During one air raid he put on his gas mask and saw himself in the mirror. 'My God,' he said. 'It's a short fat man from Mars.' And despite the constant threat of gas attack, the Israelis too saw the lighter side. One minister was interviewed by the CNN network wearing a gas mask, and members of an audience were shown calmly watching a concert during an air raid wearing their masks. Dr Ruth Westheimer, the sex counsellor who had arrived from the United States to show solidarity, declared helpfully that 'sex was no good in a gas mask'.

The allied air command, meanwhile, had the task of destroying Scuds. 'It's like looking for a needle in a haystack,' said Schwarzkopf. Lieutenant-General Thomas Kelly at the Pentagon pointed out there were 170,000 square miles in Iraq, and 'you can hide a lot in that space'. Pentagon officials began to call it the 'wild Scud chase' and moaned that they were wasting valuable resources chasing weapons which posed about as much threat as being hit by lightning. One problem was that they did not know how many mobile Scud launchers Saddam possessed. Early predictions had

estimated about forty but the true figure was much higher, possibly 150. They were unsure how many had been converted into the al-Hussein or al-Abbas versions, which had smaller payloads but the range to strike Tel Aviv and Riyadh.

The hunt was also hindered by bad weather and the Iraqis' ability to hide the launchers under bridges or in bunkers while deceiving the allied aircraft into attacking 'dud Scuds', decoys made of wood or plastic. Each evening in Riyadh, Chuck Horner, in charge of the air campaign, called together a group of experts to discuss how they could destroy more Scuds. They came up with a number of ploys: a satellite was dedicated to spotting launchers, sending back information in 'real time' to give the allied aircraft a chance of getting to the launch site in time. The Americans started using their experimental JSTARS aircraft, which had a special radar to detect movement on the ground. The AWACS, an airborne control station for aircraft, could also give early warning of a Scud launch. But the problem was getting allied aircraft to the site before the launcher had moved to a new location. The other scheme was to send in special forces to find and destroy the launchers. It was a slow campaign, and meanwhile the Scuds kept coming.

A funeral in Tel Aviv for a
victim of a Scud attack
(Amir Weinberg–Sipa/Rex)

At least Israel now had the new wonder weapon of
the war, the Patriot. This had proved its worth in Saudi
Arabia on January 20, when Patriots shot down all eight
Scud missiles fired at Riyadh and Dhahran, a main entry
point for allied weaponry into Saudi Arabia. The Patriot
became a talisman for allied forces; in one hotel lobby a
chunk of the anti-missile missile had a place of honour
and inscription reading 'We love you'. After the drama
of the air raids over Baghdad, the worldwide television
audience was being treated to a new video game:
Missile Wars. Night after night, the skies over Israel and
Saudi Arabia were lit by streaks of light as Patriots
soared off to intercept Scuds. People gave up hiding
in bunkers and went on to the rooftops to enjoy the
spectacle.

But the Patriot was not infallible. Just as the mayor of
Tel Aviv was holding a champagne party to celebrate
the apparent end of the threat, a Scud landed on the city.
A block of flats was demolished, three elderly people
died – apparently from shock and heart attacks – and
ninety-eight were injured. The attack ended the mood of
euphoria. Again there was talk of Israeli retaliation, and
scepticism over the wonder weapon. But gradually the
campaign seemed to be working, though Saddam still
managed to fire eighty-one Scuds. By the end he was
using second-rate missiles which broke up in flight. It
was one of these that was to claim the heaviest loss of
life of the Scud wars. On February 25, it hit a makeshift
barracks in Dhahran, killing twenty-eight American
soldiers. The terror weapon had lived up to its name.

An American soldier stands in front of his Patriot launcher outside Tel Aviv. The Patriot rapidly became the wonder weapon of the war after it consistently struck incoming Scud missiles. Though effective, there were concerns that the Scud warheads were still getting through and exploding. The missile was originally designed to shoot down aircraft, but was modified to attack incoming missiles using a sophisticated phased array radar guidance system (Jon Jones/Katz)

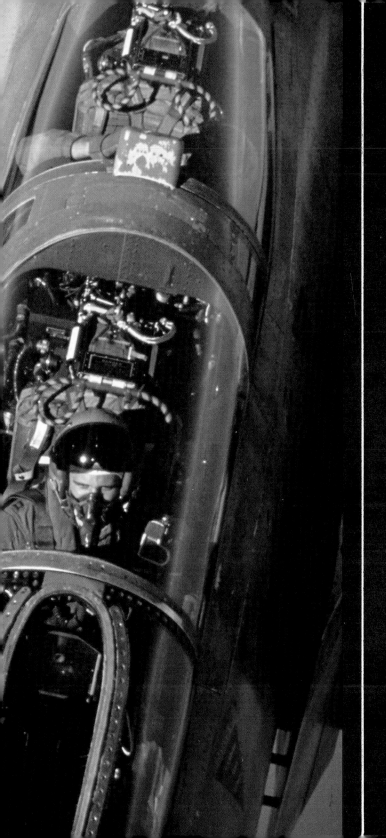

THE
AIR
WAR

WITH tongues of fire flickering from the engines of his Tornado GR1, Ian Long took off soon after midnight for one of the first low-level raids of Operation Desert Storm. A 25-year-old pilot with 3l Squadron – nicknamed the Gold Stars – he had strapped beneath the belly of his plane two JP233 runway-busting bombs, great brutes that made the plane 'fly like a brick'. And with a Walther PPK pistol under his arm, he was feeling a heady mix of fear and excitement.

Like almost all other allied pilots who climbed from airfields across Saudi Arabia and from carriers in the Gulf and Red Sea that night, he had never flown a real combat mission before. He had had no idea whether he would survive, or how he would react under fire. On paper Iraqi air defences were formidable, crammed with Soviet and French-made missiles. Long cheerfully admitted later that it was the most frightening moment of his life. He would no doubt have been even more alarmed had he known that the allies were expecting to

Far left: A Tornado is cooled by a bucket of water being poured over the fuselage. In all, the RAF – which had 60 Tornados and Jaguars in the Gulf – flew 4,000 combat sorties and dropped 3,000 tons of bombs, including 100 JP233 runway-busting bombs. It amounted to about five per cent of the allied bombing effort (Roger Hutchings/Katz)

Left: A heavily-armed French Jaguar taxis before take-off. An Anglo-French fighter-bomber, it was often armed with Hunting cluster bombs, Matra Magic missiles and 23mm cannon. It was capable of flying at over 1,000mph. At first the French had declined to bomb Iraq, and opted to limit their raids to Kuwait. But that policy soon changed, and they were active in the bombing of troops and armoured vehicles in the Kuwaiti Theatre of Operations (Gilles Bassignac– Gamma/FSP)

lose 150 planes in the air war. Given the Tornados' precarious low-flying mission, the odds were that his would be one of them.

Long flew to near the border with Iraq, where he refuelled from a converted RAF VC-10 tanker. Peeling off in the clear, dark night, and maintaining radio silence, he and the other Tornados crossed the border 'very fast and very low'. Jerry Gegg, his laconic navigator, sat behind him, guiding them to their target, an airfield deep inside Iraq. It was a tense journey flying at 500 mph a couple of hundred feet above the desert, accompanied by the roar of the engines and the occasional glint of another Tornado. Their thoughts were only on the airfield and the 'Triple A' they would meet. As they approached, they could see the anti-aircraft fire and the explosions caused by the lead Tornados. Long and Gegg were the last to go in, the most dangerous mission because the Iraqis had now been alerted and knew from which direction the Tornados were coming. The sky to the right erupted with blasts of white and yellow anti-aircraft fire as they

A Grumman EA-6B
Prowler is guided toward
steam catapults before
take off from a carrier.
Note the radiation sign o
its nosecone. The Prowle
an electronic counter-
measures aircraft packed

high-tech equipment, capable of deceiving and disrupting enemy communications. played a crucial role in preventing radar-guided surface-to-air missiles being fired at allied warplanes. With a crew of four, it has a range of 2,400 miles and a speed of 480 knots. One fighter-bomber pilot said that it 'has been so important that I would not go on a run without one.' (Associated Press)

started their bombing run. This was the worst moment. In war, pilots regard bomb release as the most nerve-wracking time; a fraction of a second, they say, seems like eternity.

After scattering the bombs along the runway, Long and Gegg ran into heavy flak again. 'As the bombs come off, you just run, run like hell,' Long said. They swung away and made their escape by flying down a wadi, one of the dried-up river beds that criss-cross the desert. It was a long and tense journey home, full of constant fear of missile attack. When they eventually made it into Saudi airspace, they could not contain themselves; they let out a spontaneous cry of joy and relief. Long returned with his face drawn from the pressure of his oxygen mask and his eyes bloodshot with fatigue. 'It was absolutely terrifying,' he said. 'It was the most scary thing I have ever done in my life. We went in low over the target – as low as we dared. We were frightened of failure, and frightened of dying.'

The mood of euphoria conveyed itself to RAF headquarters in Riyadh, where Ian Macfadyen, the chief of staff, was moved sufficiently to quote Shakespeare's lines from Henry V before the Battle of Agincourt. 'We few, we happy few, we band of brothers,' he said. 'For he today that sheds his blood with me shall be my brother . . . And gentlemen in England now abed shall think themselves accursed they were not here.' They were stirring words, and ones that may not have been shared by the RAF pilots as the force began to lose plane after plane, suffering relatively the heaviest losses of the air war.

Long and Gegg's relief at surviving was a feeling experienced by many of the 2,000 allied aircrews who flew over Iraq that first night and day of the war. Though they caught the Iraqis off guard, dropping 2,230 tons of bombs, there was intense anti-aircraft fire in places. One Wild Weasel pilot had no less than six Sams fired at him at once, and only escaped by doing frantic turns. But instead of losing dozens of aircraft, one plane came down, an American F-18. It seemed almost too easy.

But even so, the losses began to mount. Within the first week, twenty allied planes were shot down, including four Tornados. There were also several near misses. A Tornado just made it back after being shot up, and a French Jaguar pilot survived with a bullet through his helmet. The RAF agonised longer than most over whether to abandon its low-level bombing of heavily-defended targets, waiting a week before it switched to high-level raids. And the losses caused much personal anguish. Squadron Leader Pablo Mason broke down in an interview after losing two Tornados from his squadron within twenty-four hours. 'There was,' he

said, 'a constant awareness that in a few seconds' time
you might not exist.'

This fear was exacerbated when the Iraqis paraded
allied pilots on television a few days after the start of the
war. In an act that showed Saddam's stunning
ineptitude, the Iraqis said they were confining some
American PoWs to strategic sites as human shields and
that the International Red Cross would be denied access.
The reaction was outrage and revulsion. 'America is
angry about this,' Bush said, and even opponents of war
began to talk about whether Saddam should be removed
forcibly from power. The pilots, too, looked as if they
had been beaten, possibly tortured. Most of the injuries
were in fact suffered during ejection. In videos shown
across the world, they denounced the war in robotic
voices, summoning ghosts from America's past by
recalling how the Vietcong had gloated over captured
PoWs. 'I condemn this aggression against peaceful
Iraq,' intoned Lieutenant Jeffrey Zaun, his eyes glazed
and his face swollen.

The parade shook up the allied pilots waiting to fly
missions. Many decided it was wise to withhold their
names from reporters in case they were shot down. They
could merely guess and worry about how their
colleagues were being treated, and it was only after the
war that the true story emerged. Many pilots did have a
bad time. One, who had parachuted onto the tanks he
had just been strafing, was saved from a brutal
execution by furious soldiers when an officer
intervened. The Iraqis shaved the head of another pilot,
blindfolded him and regularly threatened to shoot him.
One was given electric shocks on his ears to force him
to make a propaganda video. The pilot showed a flash of
humour about his predicament by calling the device a
'Talkman'. All the PoWs were kept in solitary
confinement and most ended up in a prison they
nicknamed the 'Baghdad Biltmore', where they were
incarcerated in tiny cells with appalling food and a hole
in the corner as a lavatory. At one time the prison was
bombed and some were buried in the rubble, but they all
survived.

The inhuman treatment they suffered was in part due
to Iraqi frustration at the devastation being inflicted
upon their country. The day after the air raids started,
General Norman Schwarzkopf gave his first briefing. It
was a *tour de force* by the man who was now known
universally as 'Stormin' Norman'. Schwarzkopf exuded
bravura, claiming eighty per cent of air raids were
successful and that Saddam was being 'decimated'. No
one at this stage knew how much damage they were
inflicting, but his mood was bullish, almost exuberant.
Nor was this a repeat of the random carpet bombing of
North Vietnam or Cambodia. It was beginning to be

Right: Richard Cheney, the US defence secretary, and Colin Powell, chairman of the Joint Chiefs of Staff, at a press conference at the Pentagon. Like Schwarzkopf, Powell was an instant success and was immediately talked about as a future vice-presidential candidate to replace Dan Quayle. The son of Jamaican parents, he had completed two tours of duty in Vietnam and had mastered the complex role of being a general who understood politics. Cheney, too, enhanced his reputation during the war. A former Congressman and Bush's second choice as defence secretary, he argued from the outset in favour of massive force against Saddam Hussein
(Gamma/FSP)

Below: Iraqi planes which had fled to Iran. It started as a trickle, but became a flood. Mig-29s, Mig-25s, Su-24s, Mirage 1s and Il-76 early warning aircraft all fled to Iran to escape the allied air onslaught. In all, 147 Iraqi aircraft safely made it to Iran, though several crashed en route or were shot down by American planes. The allies at first believed it was a revolt led by air force officers, but soon concluded it was a plan by Saddam to save his planes from destruction. The scheme backfired when the Iranians refused to release the aircraft
(Gamma-FSP)

General Norman Schwarzkopf, commander of Operation Desert Storm, was a master of press briefings, in turn gruff and compassionate. At 6ft 3ins and 17 stone, his bull head sat on top of a body with the reassuring dimensions of a refrigerator. Schwarzkopf, 56, served two tours in Vietnam, winning three Silver Stars, three Bronze Stars, a DSM and two Purple Hearts; he once helped rescue a soldier who had lost a leg in a minefield. Known to be short-tempered and demanding, he at first alarmed the British in Saudi Arabia by his gung-ho appearance. But they were soon reassured that it hid an intelligent and able commander. The son of a retired general who led the police investigation into the sensational kidnapping of Charles Lindbergh's baby, Schwarzkopf was brought up in Iran and Europe before going to West Point military academy. Desert Storm was his plan, winning him acclaim in the United States, where his name became synonymous with barn-storming solutions to problems. His manner and confidence spread throughout the US military. Asked by reporters what sort of leader he was, he replied: 'I am magnificent'.

apparent that technology had all but transformed the face of war.

There had been some signs already with reports from Baghdad of pinpoint accuracy, with cruise missiles hitting a target a few yards wide after flying 500 miles, and laser-guided bombs doing almost no damage to surrounding buildings. But now the public was to be treated to first-hand evidence of the efficiency of the wonder weapons. Lieutenant General Chuck Horner, echoing the tone of his boss, produced extraordinary videos taken by pilots which showed bombs disappearing down targets as small as ventilation shafts. Introducing one tape, he said 'this is my counterpart's headquarters in Baghdad. Keep your eye on all sides of the building.'

In slow motion, a laser-guided bomb could be seen entering the shaft on the roof of air force headquarters, blowing it apart from inside. The audience gasped; here was high-tech wizardry at its alluring best. It was reinforced by the pilots. A commander of a Stealth squadron boasted: 'You pick precisely which target you want: the men's room or the ladies' room.' Soon TV audiences were watching through the bomb aimer's cross hairs, seeing bombs career through doorways, windows and on to bridges. Far below, vehicles could be seen scurrying from targets moments before they were blown apart. The 'Norm and Chuck Show', as it was soon dubbed, was a box-office hit.

It was, of course, only part of the story. No videos were shown of the misses, and though nine out of ten precision-guided weapons hit their targets, some went astray. The RAF had a video of a laser-guided bomb veering off course and exploding in a town during an attack on a bridge over the Euphrates at Fallujah. In an American raid, a rush-hour crowd was caught on a bridge and at least 50 were killed. Nor did the public see the 'video nasties'. These were scenes filmed by cameras in the noses of 'smart' missiles. One revealed the look of terror on a lorry driver's face a fraction of a second before he was killed while crossing a bridge. Another showed a panic-stricken airman racing for his shelter before he was blown apart. Of all the hundreds of thousands of bombs dropped on Iraq, fewer than one in ten was precision-guided. Seventy per cent of the remaining 'dumb' bombs missed. Even so, anyone who saw the burnt-out vehicles on the battlefield could not help but be impressed by the havoc created by the thirty per cent which struck home.

The ebullient Riyadh briefings and equally stylish ones in Washington by Richard Cheney, the defence secretary, and Colin Powell, chairman of the Joint Chiefs of Staff, created so much euphoria that the public began to believe that the war was all but over. Alarmed

US Marine pilots study a map showing their targets. Behind them is an AV-8B jump jet, the American version of the British Harrier. The AV-8B was used in ground support roles, dropping Rockeye cluster bombs. It is able to carry 16 500-pound bombs, or 12 cluster bombs. In one engagement on February 3, four AV-8Bs claimed to have destroyed 25 Iraqi tanks (Mark Peter-Sipa/ Rex)

at the mood, the military suddenly tried to appear gloomy, predicting that it could go on for some time and warning of the perils of the land war. Bush, conscious of the political dangers, also warned that 'there will be losses, there will be obstacles along the way. War is never cheap or easy.' Too much optimism, he reasoned, could lead to a rapid swing in public mood when inevitable setbacks came. Allied commanders began talking about the necessity of at least 100,000 missions before the land assault could start.

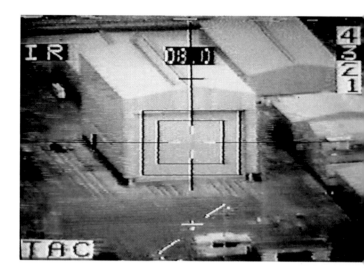

One problem was that no one could agree on how much damage they were inflicting on the Iraqis. The commanders in Riyadh were more optimistic than the conservative analysts in Washington, who relied largely on satellite intelligence. Riyadh added to this evidence from aircraft surveillance and pilots' reports. The CIA, in particular, began to challenge claims by Central Command – or Centcom – that most of the Iraqi airfields had been badly damaged. They also disputed BDA – Battle Damage Assessments – which showed Iraqi armour being steadily smashed. There was a joke in Riyadh that the CIA would only admit to a tank having been damaged if its turret was seen to be several hundred yards from the rest of the vehicle. At one time senior officers in Saudi Arabia were claiming that up to thirty per cent of tanks and artillery had been destroyed while the CIA estimated that it was fewer than ten per cent. The magic figure was fifty per cent, when it was thought safe to send in ground troops and suffer minimal losses.

At least they could agree about who was winning the air war. The Iraqi air force had barely appeared, and when it did it was shot down with monotonous regularity. About twenty Iraqi aircraft were 'splashed' in the first twenty-four hours. One even crashed into the ground after trying to shoot down an unarmed EF-111A Raven. After that they wisely, if not heroically, decided to lie low. Some fled north to remote airstrips or cowered among houses in civilian areas. Their hardened shelters, built at great expense by western contractors, were systematically obliterated. The allies had air superiority within the first few minutes of the war. Within two weeks they claimed air supremacy, allowing them to roam the skies at will.

This triumph in the air was greatly accelerated by the mysterious mass defection of the Iraqi air force to Iran. On January 26, American AWACS planes detected Iraqi planes making a dash for the Iranian frontier. The allies were baffled, and there was a suggestion it could have been due to a rebellion by the air force, or that Saddam was intent on saving his best planes and pilots for the land battle. But there were contradictory signs. The planes, which included the finest from the Iraqi air

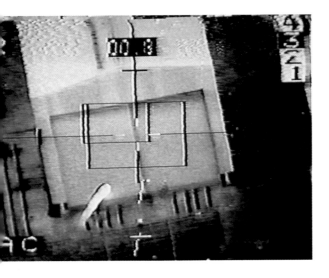

A sequence of video shots showing a hardened Iraqi hangar being blown up. Of Iraq's 594 aircraft shelters, 375 were destroyed or badly damaged in air raids, wrecking 141 enemy aircraft. The total of confirmed Iraqi aircraft destroyed in the war was 234. In all, 109,876 missions were flown by allied aircraft before the ceasefire.

Below: A group of allied pilots walk back for a debriefing, discussing their encounters with Iraqi aircraft (Chris Harris/*The Times*)

Squadron Leader Tony Paxton flying his Tornado F-3 low over the desert. A Sidewinder missile can be seen under the wing of his aircraft. Paxton was a veteran of 2,000 Tornado sorties (Steve Bent/Katz Pictures)

force, seemed frequently to be flown by novices. When attacked by allied aircraft, they took no evasive action and were shot down with ease. On one occasion an American plane pursued an Iraqi aircraft into Iranian air space before destroying it. Other Iraqi pilots just flew until their fuel ran out and then bailed out. Some could not even master a landing, and crashed.

But many did make it, and within a week more than 100 of Iraq's top Mirage 1s, SU-24s and Mig-29s were safely parked at airfields in Iran. By the end of the war 147 had sought sanctuary across the border. No one was sure whether Iran had agreed to this in advance, but it seems likely they had not. Either way it meant one less problem for the allies. The Iranians said the planes would not be handed over until hostilities had ceased, and that seemed to put an end to the affair. Even so, allied commanders kept a close watch on Iran just in case the Iranians changed their minds and allowed the Iraqi air force to seek a fleeting moment of glory.

The mass defection had made the task that much easier for the bombers as they flew their average of 2,500 missions a day. The campaign, masterminded by Chuck Horner and Brigadier General Buster Glosson, the principal target planner, was systematically grinding the Iraqis into the sand. Working from the Black Hole, a large cellar underneath the Royal Saudi Air Force headquarters in Riyadh which was crammed with computers, maps and radar screens, the Americans were slowly working through a list of hundreds of targets. It was a campaign that had been planned in meticulous detail since the late summer of 1990 when Glosson gathered a team of intelligence and surveillance experts. They knew they had a 'mother of jobs' when they realised they had to co-ordinate 1,200 strike aircraft from several nations and attack so many targets. The strategy, however, became clear when Glosson hung up a large sign saying THE WAY HOME IS THROUGH BAGHDAD. The planners' first task was to decide how air power could meet the objectives of driving Saddam out of Kuwait and destroying his ability to threaten the region. The senior officers had learned the lessons of Vietnam the hard way, and they were not going to make the same mistakes. 'I think we all learned a lesson in the last major conflict we were all involved in,' said Lieutenant General Calvin Waller, Schwarzkopf's deputy. 'You ought to make a clear-cut decision on what it is you need in order to be victorious. Then go for it.'

They opted for massive and continual strikes; an aerial blitzkrieg. It was an adaptation of AirLand Battle, the strategy for fighting the Warsaw Pact in central Europe. Their aim was to seize control of the air, taking out airfields, radars and command and control centres in the first few minutes of war. Once they had air

Top: Ian Long, aged 25, a Tornado flight lieutenant, who bombed an Iraqi airfield on the first night of the war. He described it as 'the most terrifying moment of my life.'

Above: Squadron Leader Pablo Mason, aged 40, was one of the most experienced Tornado pilots, with 18 years of flying fighter-bombers. After two of his Tornados` were lost, he said: 'I've shed more tears in the last 40 days than in the last 40 years.'

Above right: Captain Ayedh al-Shamrani, aged 30, the Saudi F-15 pilot who shot down two Iraqi Mirage F-1s as they headed towards British ships in the northern Gulf. An AWACS early-warning aircraft steered al-Shamrani in for the kill while keeping US navy planes at bay. A Pentagon spokesman said 'we wanted the Saudis to have a success. Getting two was a bonus.' (Chip Hires–Gamma/ FSP)

Right: A Tornado pilot waits anxiously in his cockpit before take-off (Chris Harris/The Times)

superiority they could remove the immediate threat to allied forces; savaging the Scuds and missile storage bunkers. Then they could pick off dangerous chemical and nuclear plants; the infrastructure – such as roads and bridges – and the troops and Republican Guards in the Kuwaiti Theatre of Operations. As General Powell said about the Iraqi army in a celebrated briefing soon after the war began, 'first we're going to cut it off, then we're going to kill it.' Schwarzkopf later added, 'What I wanted to do was break the spirit of the Republican Guard, because the spirit of the Republican Guard is the spirit of the Iraqi army.'

Crucially, Horner was given the authority to wage an integrated air campaign using all the allied aircraft. There were going to be no conflicts of interests and no conflicting orders. 'We were,' as Glosson said, 'all

singing from the same sheet of music.' The air force was determined that air power alone could win this war, and they set out to prove it.

The first problem was finding out where everything was. Human intelligence about Iraq was poor, so they had to resort to satellites and high-flying TR-1s to scan the country for anything suspicious. Special forces were sent in to gather intelligence, kidnap officers and steal anti-aircraft batteries. Foreigners who had undertaken building projects in Iraq were questioned and plans of airfields, bunkers, and buildings studied. The aim was to attack round the clock, using everything from vintage B-52s to cruise missiles. Cruise had had a difficult adolescence, with many detractors on Capitol Hill, but in this war it was to come of age. Together with laser-guided 'smart' bombs, it was to prove that modern

Below: Flight Lieutenant John Peters, aged 29, was paraded on Iraqi television on January 20 after the engine of his Tornado GR1 caught fire during a bombing raid on the first day of the war. Peters, who was almost incoherent, appeared to have been beaten up, but his injuries resulted from ejection and a bad parachute landing. He was held captive in Baghdad and was eventually freed on March 4 (Colorific)

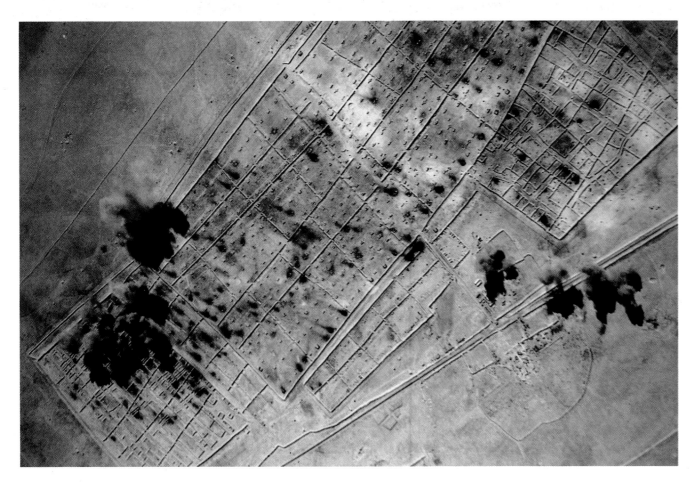

weaponry could be used to save thousands of civilian lives. Iraq and Kuwait were hit with far more precision bombs in forty-three days than Vietnam was in eight years of war, and the result was many fewer civilian casualties.

Given the vagaries of war, the campaign was unnerving in that almost everything went right. At times it almost became a victim of its own success. The bombing was so intense, with 110,000 missions, that the allies nearly ran out of munitions. Some pilots could not find enough targets to hit. At one time it was thought it could all be achieved in ten days, but resources had to be devoted to Scud-hunting, and poor weather was a hindrance. So many planes were involved, and the planning of missions was so complicated, that extra computers had to be brought in to produce a daily flight menu as thick as a telephone directory. Otherwise it was a model campaign, albeit against a far-inferior enemy. General Merrill McPeak, the United States' air force's chief of staff, claimed after the war was over that this was 'the first time in history that a field army has been defeated by air power.'

And defeated it clearly was. The bombing had a huge physical and psychological impact on the Iraqi troops. It was so intense and so terrifying that up to 200,000 soldiers may have deserted during the five weeks of the air campaign. In some units desertions exceeded casualties by ten to one. No one is certain how many died or were injured. 'They were under constant bombardment twenty-four hours a day, five weeks in a row without a let-up,' an American general said. 'No one has ever had to experience that in the history of warfare. It's no wonder the place was coming unglued at the seams.' Many undoubtedly died under the bombing and were buried deep in the sands; like some victims of the First World War, their remains may be lost forever. Tanks were being spotted with infra-red detectors and being killed at the rate of 100 a day. Their response was to dig deeper, until they all but disappeared beneath the sand. Some crews were even buried alive as they sought to escape the relentless pounding.

Another well-placed source added that 'we probably killed more than 100,000 people without ever occupying the territory. We passed over them day after day. It was a different kind of war to one we've ever fought.' It was particularly different in that during the

A cormorant struggles through thick crude oil in the northern Gulf. The deliberate leakage of vast quantities of oil into the Gulf was first detected a week after the start of the war. It was thought Saddam had authorised the move partially as an act of defiance – 'Eco-terrorism' – and partly to deter an amphibious landing. The oil from a terminal and the hulls of tankers moved steadily south, ravaging wildlife and clogging the desalination plants which supplied fresh water to Saudi Arabia. The slick was at first thought to be vast – 11 million barrels – but this was later greatly scaled down to 1.5 million barrels, nonetheless still making it six times bigger than the Exxon Valdez spill off Alaska. The leakage was stopped by precision-bombing raids, but the Iraqis leaked more oil into Gulf waters at a later stage and in a final act of revenge set fire to Kuwait's oil wells (Mike Moore–*Today*)

first four weeks of the air war, the Americans lost just fourteen dead and twelve wounded. No one wanted to say it out loud, but it looked remarkably like the 'turkey shoot' some had predicted at the outset of the crisis.

Those Iraqis who deserted to allied lines were able to convey some of the horror of the air offensive, but one of the most compelling accounts came from the diary of an unknown platoon commander found by American troops in a bunker three miles from the Kuwaiti border. Seen by a reporter from the *Los Angeles Times*, the diary revealed the fear and frustration of being bombed day after day by planes out of reach of Iraqi guns. The man was clearly a loyal officer. On January 15, the day of the UN deadline for Iraqi withdrawal, he wrote of the 'imperialist American-Zionist alliance' confronting

Iraq. Two days later the bombs began to fall. The platoon had its first lucky escape when a bunker it had just moved out of was blown apart. The next day they watched in awe as explosions continued for an hour at a nearby ammunition dump. On January 19 a bomb landed next to the platoon but did not explode. By now they were short of food and water, ignored by an indifferent high command. 'But God's kindness hasn't left us alone, for it started to rain heavily and we collected enough water to drink, cook and wash,' he wrote.

It was only a brief respite. On January 23 'very large' shrapnel from bombs fell everywhere and the next day they saw B-52s high above them. Heavy cloud prevented them from being bombed. The platoon

his gas stove to turn it off and 'a flame came up and burnt my moustache and my hair. I adjusted it accordingly,' he wrote. It was the last entry in the diary.

Though the air force was crushed and the army pounded, the Iraqis were not yet ready to give up. Just as the allied troops were beginning to wonder whether a land offensive would be necessary, Saddam delivered one of his surprises. On January 30, under a full moon, the 'demoralised and defeated' Iraqi army invaded Saudi Arabia at three points, possibly in search of intelligence after being 'blinded' by the air assault. At al-Wafra, twenty T-55 tanks and 400 men caught the allies by surprise and fought a fierce engagement. It was here that eleven Americans in armoured personnel carriers were killed accidentally by one of their own helicopters.

But the main assault came at the abandoned border town of Khafji. Buoyed by earlier defections, the few allied troops guarding the town at first thought the armour rumbling towards them was just another defection on a spectacular scale. Certainly the Iraqi tanks had their guns pointing behind them, a sign that they did not intend to fight. But fight they did, and in the process gave the allies a serious fright. The main thrust came soon after midnight when a column of T-55 tanks and armoured personnel carriers, with 3,000 to 4,000 troops, broke through the border and sped down the eight-mile metalled highway to Khafji. It took just twenty minutes to reach the town and dispose of a Saudi roadblock. There was an engagement with some Saudi national guardsmen and US troops, but then another armoured column roared into town and took control of the north-eastern quarter. The Iraqis had successfully occupied a small corner of Saudi Arabia. One journalist telephoned the Beach Hotel and was answered by a jubilant Iraqi soldier who was helping himself to breakfast from the hotel's supplies. 'We are Saddam's soldiers,' he announced proudly, adding optimistically: 'See you in Jerusalem.'

For the next thirty-six hours this unobtrusive little seaside town was to witness the fiercest engagement of the war. Luckily for the Americans – if not the men concerned – two reconnaissance teams of Marines were trapped on the upper floors of a deserted building and could direct fire onto Iraqi positions. The Iraqis, for their part, had placed some observers on top of a water tower and were able to direct uncomfortably accurate fire on Saudi troops. Richard Ellis, a *Sunday Times* war reporter in Saudi Arabia, was one of the few journalists who got inside the town while fighting was still going on. He found that it was much tougher than the briefers had been admitting in Riyadh, and that the battle went on longer than anyone had expected.

commander began to write longingly of his five-day pass, which was due to start on January 31. On January 28, fifteen aircraft attacked them at dawn and one bomb landed very close. 'Thank God, nobody was hit,' he wrote in a refrain that appeared regularly in the diary. On this occasion, air raids went on all day and all night, raining shrapnel on their heads as they huddled in their dug-outs and bunkers. The B-52s and F-15s, however, were flying too low and were driven away by Iraqi ground fire. The next day the Americans returned having learnt their lesson; F-18s and F-14s bombed them from high altitude, out of range of the guns. Later that day they saw F-16s flying overhead, apparently taking photographs of battle damage. It was a bad day all round. After breakfast, the lieutenant reached over

The allies knew, however, that they had to eject the Iraqis quickly. In the end the Saudis, with American air and artillery assistance, were able to triumph within a couple of days, but not before they took several casualties in house-to-house fighting. Whatever Schwarzkopf might say about it being like 'a mosquito biting an elephant', the foray was an embarrassment. It led to a reassessment of the 'flea-bitten members of the beer-belly brigade', which until then had been the popular view held by British troops. For thirty-six hours the Iraqis fought with courage and ferocity, and in the process reversed some cherished notions about how they would battle when the allies launched the invasion to liberate Kuwait. Nor did it seem the end of Iraqi aggression. Saddam followed Khafji with a large-scale manoeuvering which seemed to herald a main offensive. All it did, however, was provide targets for allied aircraft.

Lieutenant Colonel Dick White, in a celebrated phrase, said it was like 'flipping on the light in the kitchen at night and the cockroaches start scurrying. It was exactly what we were looking for.' Saddam's attempt to seize the initiative had run into a problem that decided the outcome; the allies had air supremacy, and they used it ruthlessly. That was not going to change, and the question was how long he could hold out in the main offensive, which was now imminent.

Left: A destroyed Iraqi armoured personnel carrier at the entrance to Khafji (Georges Merillon–Gamma/FSP)

Above: Saudi troops celebrate their victory after intense fighting (Christopher Morris–Black Star/Colorific)

Darkness at Noon: A dense cloud of smoke blackens the midday sky of Khafji on February 22 as huge fires from burning Kuwaiti oil wells – set ablaze by the Iraqi army – obliterate the sun. President Bush said that Saddam Hussein was 'wantonly setting fire to and destroying oil wells' in a scorched earth campaign even before the land war had begun.

At first the pollution seemed dreadful, spreading as far as the Himalayas and Turkey. Temperatures dropped and the old and young suffered from chest complaints. No one could be sure of the long-term effects, but some environmentalists and anti-war activists predicted that the smoke would rise to the stratosphere and cause global cooling, a form of nuclear winter. That in turn would lead to a disruption of the monsoon, the failure of crops and mass starvation.

Although the pollution was clearly serious regionally, this appeared to be a gross exaggeration. Scientists detected only traces of the smoke in the stratosphere, with most lingering at about 6,000 feet. They noted that the average size of the smoke particles was 0.3 microns, an ideal size for absorbing sunlight. Some British scientists decided it was ten times worse than London on a busy day. They predicted that acid rain, black snow and other noxious chemicals would keep falling over the region, but the environmental damage would be limited (Frederick Stevens–Sipa/Rex)

THE
100 HOUR
WAR

GENERAL Norman Schwarzkopf is a keen military historian. At West Point, and ever since, he has studied war with a sharp eye for the lessons for today. His favourite battle, for its sheer conceptual cunning, was Hannibal's great victory over the Romans at Cannae in 216BC. But Schwarzkopf is also a realist. He experienced defeat personally in Vietnam, where he was made painfully aware how wars could be lost by great nations. He also knew that wars can be won by planning and deception.

As Schwarzkopf pondered in late 1990 how to defeat Saddam Hussein and his vast army, his mind turned to another great tank battle in the desert, the British victory at El Alamein where Montgomery's 8th army put an end to German ambitions in North Africa and the Middle East. Schwarzkopf re-read the history of the campaign, and it gave him an idea. 'One of the things the British did extremely well was a deception operation that caused the Germans to think the main attack was going to come someplace else,' he said. If his aim was to save lives and crush Saddam's army swiftly, there was a lesson here.

He set about applying it to the Gulf with the relentless energy and impatience for which he was becoming famous. Much to the irritation of the US Marines, he decided from the outset not to have an amphibious landing. It was reckoned that the human cost of an Iwo Jima-style operation would be too high, and that the mere threat of a seaborne invasion would tie down several Iraqi divisions, thus achieving its objective. All the practice landings, the deployment of thousands of Marines to ships, the placing of those ships off the coast of Kuwait and the bombardment of the shoreline defences by the 16-inch guns of the great battleships were an elaborate bluff. This was the first deception.

But it got Schwarzkopf thinking. Each week he was made painfully aware of how Saddam was reinforcing Kuwait with men and equipment, how they were digging in with their chemical weapons and artillery behind berms, ramparts, oil-filled trenches, minefields and barbed wire. He knew that Saddam had only one chance of victory; to shackle allied forces to killing zones and bombard them as they struggled to breach the defences. As Schwarzkopf said: 'Saddam must have thought we were going to fight him the way the Iranians did. He thought we were going to have one or two days of preparation and then we were going to come in mass attacks across the ground into his fire trenches and barbed wire and minefields. His soldiers were going to fall back and they were going to attrit us and attrit us, and about the time we got to the middle of Kuwait and we were severely weakened, he was going to unleash the Republican Guard from the northern border and they

Left and previous pages: The Desert Rats prepare for war. The Royal Regiment of Fusiliers, part of the 4th Armoured Brigade, form their Warrior armoured personnel carriers into a battle group just before crossing into Iraq on February 24. The 4th Armoured Brigade, led by Brigadier Christopher Hammerbeck, also included the 14th/20th King's Hussars armoured regiment with Challenger tanks, and the Royal Scots using Warriors. There were several other key units – artillery, engineers, Army Air Corps and air defence – which made up the brigade.

The other British armoured brigade was the 7th, led by Brigadier Patrick Cordingley, whose 110 Challengers, 60 Warriors and self-propelled M-109s destroyed 90 Iraqi tanks, 80 armoured vehicles, 30 artillery pieces, and took 2,800 prisoners. The brigade estimated that about 120 Iraqis were killed in combat with the unit, while it lost four dead and 15 wounded. The brigade included the Queen's Royal Irish Hussars, the Royal Scots Dragoon Guards and 1st Battalion, the Staffordshire Regiment. Reconnaissance units of the 16th/5th The Queen's Royal Lancers and The Queen's Dragoon Guards moved ahead of the brigades.

Both brigades formed the British 1st Armoured Division, under the command of Major General Rupert Smith. The division covered more than 200 miles during the war with American units and the VII Corps and destroyed 300 Iraqi tanks, more than 100 armoured vehicles and about 100 artillery pieces (Mike Moore/*Today*)

Corporal Blash of B Company, the Royal Scots, prays in the desert at the last service before G-Day (Mike Moore/*Today*)

Far right: A tank squadron from the 7th Armoured Brigade near the border with Iraq waits for war (Mike Moore/*Today*)

were going to come screaming down and counter-attack and kill us all.'

It was not an amusing concept, and one that Schwarzkopf had no intention of permitting. Discounting a direct attack on Kuwait City, he looked for an alternative. As he watched the Iraqi buildup near the coast, a plan evolved to attack through western Kuwait, avoiding the main defences and stopping short of the 120,000 troops of the Republican Guard, who straddled the Iraqi-Kuwaiti northern border. The aim was to tempt the Guard out of its well-fortified positions, and pummel it from the air.

But Saddam kept extending his defences in western Kuwait, and gradually that scheme lost its attraction. Then in October, as the general sat musing over his maps, the great plan occurred to him, one of such compelling simplicity that he was surprised it had not struck him earlier. It was to swing a huge armoured 'left hook' from the west that would knock Saddam sideways. Schwarzkopf recalled how the Iraqi defences were 'getting thicker and thicker, and heavier and heavier. But it

President George Bush and James Baker, his secretary of state and close friend, discuss a Soviet peace plan in the Oval Office at the White House just days before the start of the ground invasion of Iraq and Kuwait. The Russians, after a period of intense diplomatic activity, detected a shift in Saddam's position after five weeks of air bombardment. He seemed to be talking about a possible withdrawal from Kuwait. The Kremlin drafted an eight-point peace proposal that appeared to meet many of Bush's conditions. But the terms of the withdrawal were too vague and too late, and few wanted Saddam to be able to withdraw with his army intact after plundering Kuwait. That would enable him to claim victory, and the next time he decided to invade a neighbour he might possess nuclear weapons. Bush had to pretend to consider the plan, while privately lobbying allied leaders to reject it. The president's attitude hardened as news emerged of Saddam's scorched earth policy, setting fire to hundreds of Kuwaiti oilwells. Bush issued tough terms which he knew Saddam would find all but unacceptable: a complete Iraqi withdrawal within seven days and a deadline of noon, Washington time, on February 23 for the pullout. It was too much for Saddam to swallow, and the land invasion started soon afterwards (Gamma/FSP)

General Norman Schwarzkopf, the allied commander, and Lieutenant General Sir Peter de la Billière, commander of the British forces in the Gulf, had an initially stormy relationship but had forged a mutual respect for each other by the time the war started. The British 1st Armoured Division moved from the coast where it had been part of a Marine force, and joined VII Corps in a massive deception operation. It became one of the spearhead heavy tank divisions to deliver the knock-out blow as part of the 'left hook' to Saddam Hussein and the Republican Guard (Associated Press/Photocolor)

Below: The first news of the allied ground offensive came in the early hours of Sunday morning in London

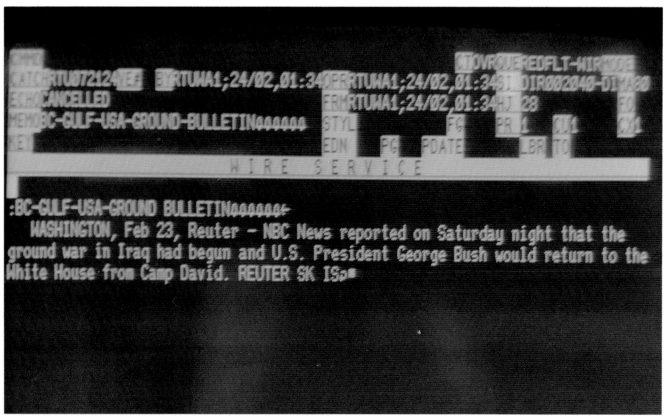

:BC-GULF-USA-GROUND BULLETIN◊◊◊◊◊◊◊
    WASHINGTON, Feb 23, Reuter — NBC News reported on Saturday night that the ground war in Iraq had begun and U.S. President George Bush would return to the White House from Camp David. REUTER SK ISa■

wasn't going any farther out to the west. So I remembered the fact that in desert warfare you can deceive your enemy as to the point of the main attack. And I said: "That's it. That's the key".'

The key was to switch the main assault, what the Germans called the *Schwerpunkt*, away from the fortifications of southern Kuwait towards the west. He could then punch his way far north, before swinging east to take the Iraqis from the flank. It looked fine on the map, but would he have the logistics to sustain such a long-range operation? The main problem was getting enough fuel and ammunition so far into Iraq. If they advanced quickly, they would cover 200 miles in two days. Schwarzkopf was aware of how General Patton in the Second World War over-extended himself trying to relieve paratroopers at Arnhem. Schwarzkopf had to be sure he could get enough fuel trucks to the region for the gas-guzzling M1A1 tanks, which could consume six gallons a minute.

The general went out to the western border region, kicked the sand and saw that it was hard enough to take supply lorries as well as heavy, tracked armour. Just to be sure, he sent special forces deep into Iraq to take soil samples and find trails for the tankers that would enable the armour to keep rolling. 'I think it never even dawned on him (Saddam) that we would ever go into Iraq,' Schwarzkopf said. 'Kuwait was the prize. And then, looking at our naval capacity, I think they thought that we were going to come driving down in through Kuwait harbour because downtown Kuwait City was the goal.'

But if the plan was to be successful, it had to be kept secret. Saddam could otherwise extend his defences westwards. The best solution, Schwarzkopf decided, was an elaborate deception scheme, which his staff set about planning from late October. Not all of them were happy with the project. 'I got a lot of guff,' said Schwarzkopf. Some of his officers, and the intelligence agencies in Washington, warned that it could all go badly wrong, that it was too ambitious. On some days Schwarzkopf awoke thinking, 'it's never going to work and we're going to lose everybody.'

But he stuck with it and won the support of Sir Peter de la Billière, the commander of British forces in the Gulf. The 1st Armoured Division at that time was meant to bludgeon its way up the coast with the Marines. But the British lobbied for and won a role in the main assault into Iraq. The French, too, 150 miles to the west of Kuwait, were given the job of storming up with elements of the US 82nd Airborne to block a counter-attack. The objective was to cut the Iraqis off with the mobile XVIII Corps, and smash them with the heavy VII Corps.

A British heavy artillery unit fires its first shots of the war as it bombards Iraqi positions. In the background is a giant sand wall bulldozed by the allies to deter an Iraqi offensive. It was the biggest artillery barrage unleashed by the British since the Second World War. The 1st Armoured Division fired 2,500 rounds of eight-inch shells and 10,000 rounds of 155mm during the softening-up operations. They also loosed off 2,500 rockets from the Multiple-Launch Rocket System, causing havoc in Iraqi positions (Ken Lennox/*Daily Mirror*)

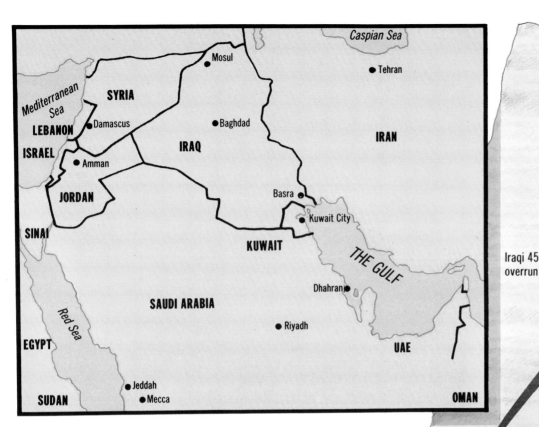

THE 100 HOUR WAR

Faced with the world's fourth largest army, formidable fortifications and more than 4,000 Iraqi tanks, General Norman Schwarzkopf opted to go wide and deep, delivering a swinging 'left hook' from the west. The result was one of the most devastating blitzkriegs in history. Within four days, 70,000 Iraqis had surrendered and the Republican Guard was broken. It was a stunning victory, cleverly conceived and brilliantly executed.

IRAQ

Iraqi 45th division overrun

Salman

Iraqi ar[...]
battalio[...]

FRENCH
6th Armoured
USA
82nd Airborne
(The All Americans)

4am Sunday
French and Americans make rapid advance with Gazelle helicopters, light AMX tanks and anti-tank squads to secure the western flank. They seize the airfield at Salman

USA
101st Airborne
(The Screaming Eagles)

8am Sunday
The Americans launch the biggest helicopter assault in history. They establish a forward fuel and supply base before thousands of troops in a single flight of 420 Blackhawks set up a base codenamed Cobra at Tallil, 10 miles south of Nasiriyah

USA
3rd Armoured Cavalry Regiment.
24th Mechanised Infantry Division

4pm Sunday
24th Mechanised heads towards Euphrates valley before swinging east to confront the Republican Guard

USA
1st Armoured.
2nd Armoured Cavalry Regiment

USA
1st Infa[...]
1st Cav[...]
BRITIS[...]
1st Arm[...]

4pm Sunday
US VII Corps, including the Briti[...] 1st armoured division, strikes north into Iraq

SAUDI ARABIA

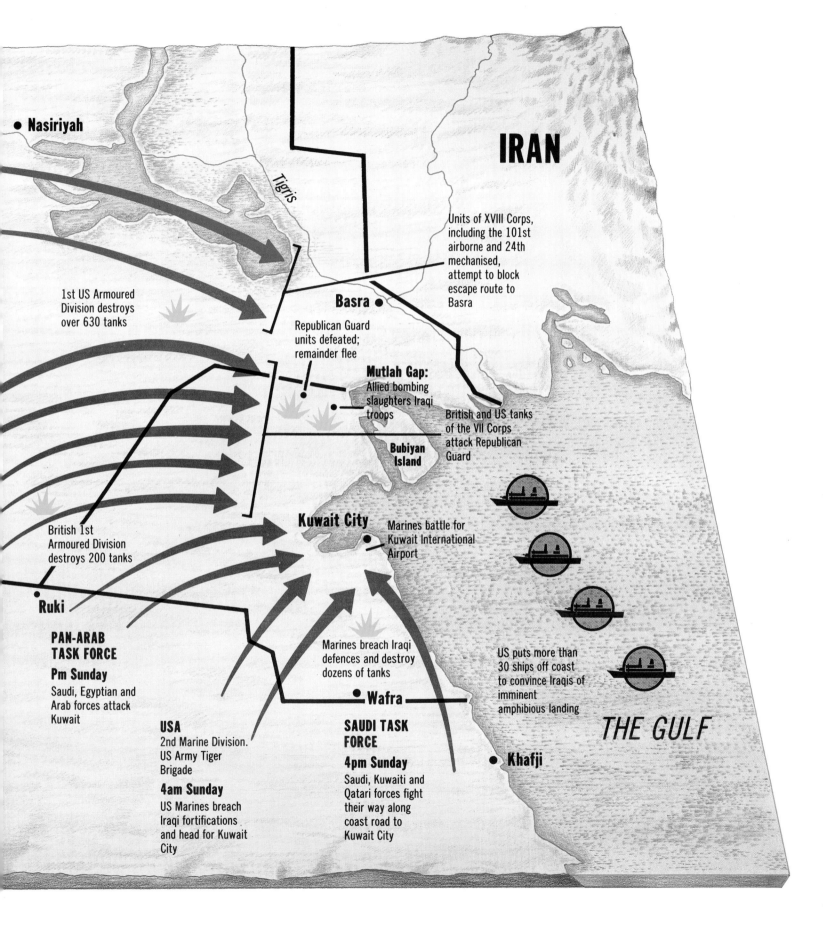

● Nasiriyah

IRAN

Tigris

Units of XVIII Corps, including the 101st airborne and 24th mechanised, attempt to block escape route to Basra

Basra ●

1st US Armoured Division destroys over 630 tanks

Republican Guard units defeated; remainder flee

Mutlah Gap: Allied bombing slaughters Iraqi troops

British and US tanks of the VII Corps attack Republican Guard

Bubiyan Island

Kuwait City

Marines battle for Kuwait International Airport

British 1st Armoured Division destroys 200 tanks

US puts more than 30 ships off coast to convince Iraqis of imminent amphibious landing

● **Ruki**

PAN-ARAB TASK FORCE

Pm Sunday

Saudi, Egyptian and Arab forces attack Kuwait

Marines breach Iraqi defences and destroy dozens of tanks

● **Wafra**

THE GULF

USA
2nd Marine Division. US Army Tiger Brigade

4am Sunday
US Marines breach Iraqi fortifications and head for Kuwait City

SAUDI TASK FORCE

4pm Sunday
Saudi, Kuwaiti and Qatari forces fight their way along coast road to Kuwait City

● **Khafji**

The allies had one big advantage over the Iraqis for the deception plan. With no satellites, a fearful air force and crude ground reconnaissance, the Iraqis had no real means of knowing what was going on. Even so, Schwarzkopf had to wait until well after the air war started on January 17 before he could consider moving his troops. By then none of the Iraqi aircraft dared venture up to find out what was happening. The Iraqis' only means of analysing allied planning was signals intelligence.

This was also the means that Schwarzkopf used to fool them. His problem was hiding the sudden removal of three and a half divisions from south of Kuwait and their equally abrupt reappearance hundreds of miles to the west. Even the Iraqis, blind as they were, might detect that. So the allies began their plan of creating 'ghost divisions' to fill the desert where they had been dug in for months. The Marines simulated the activities of a full division by keeping a headquarters running with busy radio traffic and helicopters flying in and out. Known as Task Force Troy – in memory of the horse – 460 men simulated the carrying-on of 16,000. The desert was dotted with dummy tanks and artillery to fool suspected Bedouin spies. The British had Rhino Force, which put out recordings from field exercises by the 1st Armoured. Loudspeakers blared out the noises of tanks and commands while the troops moved west. It was an entertaining extravaganza with a deadly serious intent.

As this was going on, Schwarzkopf moved 150,000

Left: Units from the French 6th Light Armoured Division race across the desert in AMX-30 B2 tanks as part of the planned flanking move in the far west to prevent an Iraqi counter-attack. They were accompanied by elements of the 82nd Airborne, one of the first units to land in France on D-Day in 1944. It was the first time that French and American units had fought together since the Korean War. France sent 16,000 ground troops to Saudi Arabia from the *Force d'Action Rapide*, a highly-skilled professional force used to desert conditions (Sipa/Rex)

Above: Egyptian units fire their multiple launch rockets at Iraqi positions along the Kuwaiti border (Delahaye– Sipa/Rex)

men westwards, some of them more than 500 miles in a matter of days along a single road. There was a seemingly endless flow of tank transporters heading for the attack zones, followed by tankers and all the other machinery of war needed to keep so many sustained for sixty days. XVIII Corps, normally 70,000-strong in Germany, doubled in size, with 23,000 vehicles. VII Corps had no fewer than 36,000 vehicles. 'This was an extraordinary move,' said Schwarzkopf. 'I can't recall any time in the annals of military history when the number of forces have moved over this distance to put themselves in a position to be able to attack.'

There were innumerable uncertainties, one of them being concern over how to transform allied troops trained for defence in Germany into stormtroopers of a tank-driven blitzkrieg. They were aware that it required a different 'mindset'. General Fred Franks, commander of VII Corps, dealt with the problem by regarding the desert as an ocean, lecturing his officers that it enabled them to imitate the quick, reflexive manoeuvres of naval warfare. This became a good-natured joke, and some of his men waited until Franks was in a van one day which served as a mobile command post and began to rock the vehicle while singing 'Anchors Aweigh.'

As the air offensive continued, the only problem was deciding the date of attack. The war was going well, and there were contradictory pressures on Schwarzkopf. Some wanted to let the air force destroy the Iraqis so thoroughly that all the ground forces had to do was mop up. That would keep casualties down and ensure support at home. But other generals were urging a quick attack, worried that the deception plan might not be working and concerned over the approaching Saudi summer and the festival of Ramadan. The men, too, were keyed up for an attack; they could not be kept waiting too long.

Schwarzkopf had other worries on top of this. Despite his sophisticated intelligence-gathering operation, he was still uncertain of Saddam's strengths and weaknesses. He had good reason to be; intelligence had grossly overestimated Iraq's numerical strength. They knew there were 42 divisions there, and assumed this meant 540,000 men. In fact, because of desertions and undermanned units, there were probably only 350,000. The allies, in contrast, had nine American divisions, one British, one French and three Arab. Schwarzkopf still assumed, incorrectly, that he was outnumbered by three to two overall, and two to one in combat troops.

Satellite pictures, too, showed defences to be stronger than they were, and intelligence reports still had the Iraqis down as good soldiers, reinforced in part by the evidence of Khafji. 'They built these guys to be monsters,' complained one Marine general. It was noted that the Iraqis had good supplies of ammunition, some

An American soldier guides a Blackhawk helicopter in to land along the Iraqi frontier. In what the Americans described as the biggest helicopter-borne assault in history, hundreds of helicopters from the 82nd Airborne and 101st Airborne swept into Iraq on G-day, February 24. Some 3,000 soldiers from the 82nd Airborne were operating with 10,500 men from France's Daguet light armoured division. The Blackhawks, indispensable workhorses and troop carriers, were also used to airlift men into the American embassy during the liberation of Kuwait City (Alex–Sipa/Rex)

Combat troops from the 101st Airborne (The Screaming Eagles) deploy for offensive operations from a Chinook helicopter. On February 24, over 300 helicopters of the 101st swept into Iraq carrying more than 2,000 troops in a 'bold, audacious action' to cut Saddam Hussein's supply lines and prevent escape from the Kuwaiti Theatre of Operations. By late afternoon, the soldiers had carved out a supply area covering 60 square miles to serve as a giant fuel and ammunition dump. The Chinooks were also used to carry vast rubber bladders of fuel to the staging area. Other helicopters brought in guns, ammunition, food, tents and vehicles slung beneath them.

Apache, Huey and Cobra attack helicopters rode shotgun to Blackhawk and Chinook aircraft along six air corridors into Iraq. Some 15,000 troops from the 101st leapfrogged from the supply base on to Nasiriyah in the Euphrates valley to cut off a retreat by the Iraqis and prevent a counter-attack (Bill Gentile–Sipa/Rex)

strong bunkers and rearguard units well stocked with food. Who was to say they would not fight to the death for the 19th province? Certainly everyone expected high allied casualties – possibly 10,000, maybe even 50,000. They were also certain the Iraqis would use chemical weapons, or 'slime' the allied troops, as the soldiers referred to it.

Against this Schwarzkopf had reports from special forces – who had been in and out of Kuwait and Iraq for months – of poor discipline and execution squads to keep the men in the front line. This was confirmed by the ever-increasing flow of deserters. The Iraqis could not even fire their artillery properly. A Marine colonel reported that 'those bastards have been shooting at me – they know where I am and they can't hit me. I don't think they're all that great.' It was enough for Schwarzkopf to say in mid-February that the Iraqi army was disintegrating and on the verge of collapse. They were losing two battalions of tanks a day, an attrition rate that no army could survive. But the general still injected a note of caution, saying they were not yet broken. He could not be sure. Though the Iraqis were being pounded daily in air raids, there was still the long-running dispute between Riyadh and Washington over the extent of damage. It was a high-risk gamble for a man who liked the odds heavily in his favour when dealing with the lives of his men. Few could forget his words just weeks before G-day: 'I don't want my soldiers to die,' he said. 'I don't want them maimed.'

But decision time was approaching, and on February 9 Richard Cheney, the defence secretary, and Colin Powell, chairman of the Joint Chiefs of Staff, visited Saudi Arabia to be briefed by the generals and decide on a date. Schwarzkopf favoured more time for the air assault and for preparing for the land war, but Cheney and Powell told him that political and diplomatic pressures meant they had to move soon.

After they had gone, Schwarzkopf called his commanders together and told them that they would recommend to President Bush that the attack should start between the 21st and 25th. No one was sure how long it would take. Most predicted anything between a week and twenty days. Even so, Schwarzkopf had laid in enough supplies for two months. Very few suspected it could all be over in four days. On February 14, Schwarzkopf set the clock running; G minus seven. Two days later, VII Corps made its move west to just north of Hafar al-Batin.

There was a last brief attempt at diplomacy, with Mikhail Gorbachev – aware the attack was imminent – seeking to broker a peace deal. But Saddam ignored tough demands from Bush and by then the Americans were fed up with prevarication. On February 21, Bush

The following sequence of pictures by Mike Moore of *Today* are some of the few action shots taken of British troops in combat during the 100 Hour War. They show an infantry attack by the men of 5 platoon, B company, The Royal Scots, who were deployed from their Warriors to destroy a Soviet-made MTLB which was holding up the advance. The soldier on the left, with sweat running down his face, is about to be called forward by his platoon commander, Sergeant Tom Gorrian, to give covering fire

The soldier advances with live fire hitting the sand in front of him. On the right, some of his colleagues take up positions before the grenade attack

Above: Sergeant Tom Gorrian, under covering fire, moves forward to get in position to throw a grenade at the target, which is already ablaze. In the picture below, the grenade can be seen in flight

Right: The phosphorous grenade explodes. Although British troops had to fight in similar skirmishes, most Iraqis were only too eager to surrender and much of the destruction was wrought by the Challenger tanks

An Iraqi tank burns in the desert. The allies destroyed no less than 3,847 of Saddam Hussein's tanks, one of the biggest concentrations of armour in history. Many were bombed from the air, but large numbers were destroyed by artillery and American and British tanks. Allied soldiers said the mainly Soviet-built tanks were hopelessly outclassed by coalition armour, especially the American M1A1 and the British Challenger, which had the Iraqis outgunned and outmanoeuvred. Many were older T-55s and T-62s, but even the more advanced T-72 fared badly against the better-trained allied troops. The crushing defeat led Soviet tacticians and manufacturers to reconsider the capabilities of their weapons. Several Iraqi tanks were dug in too deeply for them to be brought out in time to meet the allied offensive. And some tank crews were reportedly buried alive in their tanks under the sand (Delahaye–Sipa/Rex)

agreed with a suggestion by Powell that Saddam be given two days, until midday on Saturday, to withdraw. The deadline passed, and Bush took the decision to send in the ground forces. He told the four living former US presidents by telephone, and informed leaders of Congress. Schwarzkopf had already decided there was no point in waiting and had opted to go in that night. The stage was now set for the biggest land invasion since D-Day.

Though the main assault began at 4am on February 24, when thousands of men and hundreds of armoured vehicles streamed across the frontiers of Iraq and Kuwait, a small invasion by the Marines had already started two days before amid great secrecy. Unnoticed by the Iraqis, Task forces Grizzly and Taro – comprising 2,000 'leathernecks' – sneaked a dozen miles into Kuwait during a night-time rainstorm. The aim of this expeditionary force was to deal with the Iraqi defences feared most by the allies: minefields and artillery. But it was the start of the liberation of Kuwait.

The task forces met no resistance that first night and spent the daylight hours dug in, cleaning their guns miles behind enemy lines. The Iraqis, it seemed, had not spotted them and there was no harassing fire. Their second piece of luck came when some Iraqis deserted to them. Pathetically grateful to the Americans for not shooting them, the deserters guided the Marines through a minefield. The desertions – even these small task forces took 540 prisoners – were a sign of what was to come. The way was now cleared for the vanguard of the Marines to punch through Iraqi defences deep into Kuwait. One Marine commander put it graphically to his men on the eve of battle: 'the toilet chain has already been pulled, and Saddam Hussein is about to be flushed away.'

One of the first Marine units over the top was Task Force Ripper, its 'grunts' in their armoured vehicles singing the Marine battle hymn and heavy metal songs. Leading one squadron was Lieutenant William Delaney, who took part in perhaps the first armoured engagement of the land war. The Marines had breached the 'impregnable' defences with ease, and were now free to manoeuvre in the desert beyond the ramparts. With a sky dark with burning oil wells, it was a Wagnerian setting for a brief but bloody battle which became a pattern for the 100-hour war.

'We destroyed them,' he recalled. 'Our company got fifteen tanks. Tanks were blowing up with tremendous explosions. Turrets flipped off. Everybody in my platoon got a tank kill. There were bodies all over the place. We just destroyed everything in front of us. If it didn't have a white flag, we shot it – trucks, vehicles, bunkers . . . the ground opened up and these guys came

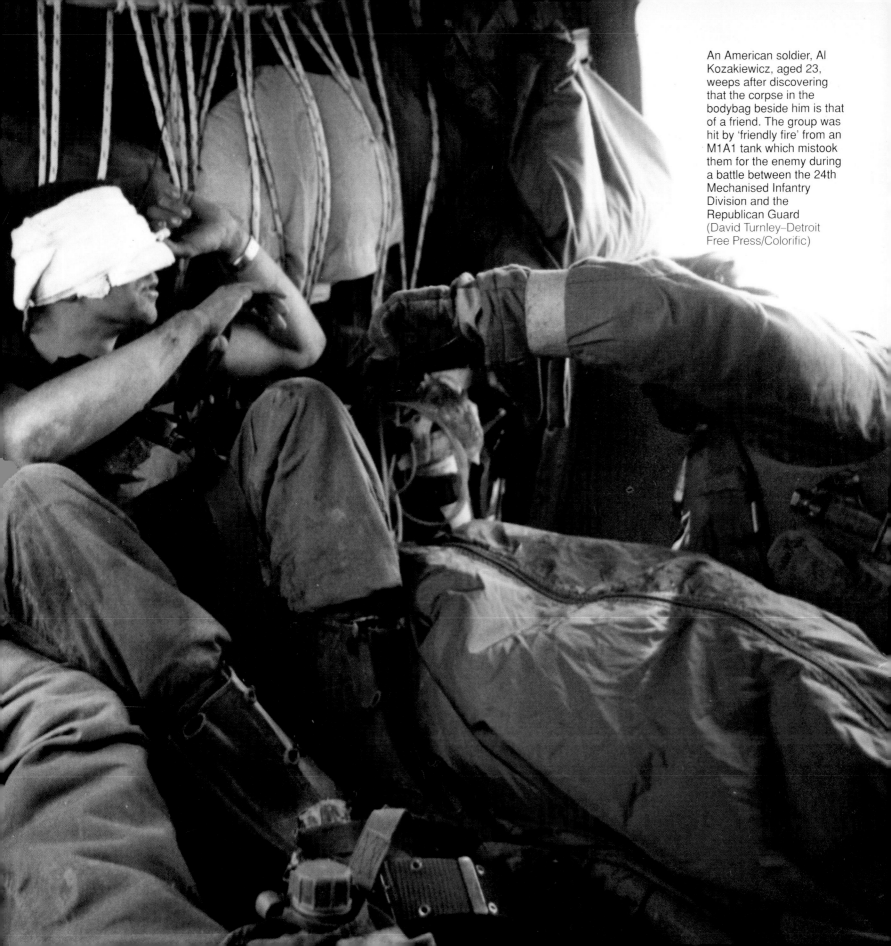

An American soldier, Al Kozakiewicz, aged 23, weeps after discovering that the corpse in the bodybag beside him is that of a friend. The group was hit by 'friendly fire' from an M1A1 tank which mistook them for the enemy during a battle between the 24th Mechanised Infantry Division and the Republican Guard (David Turnley–Detroit Free Press/Colorific)

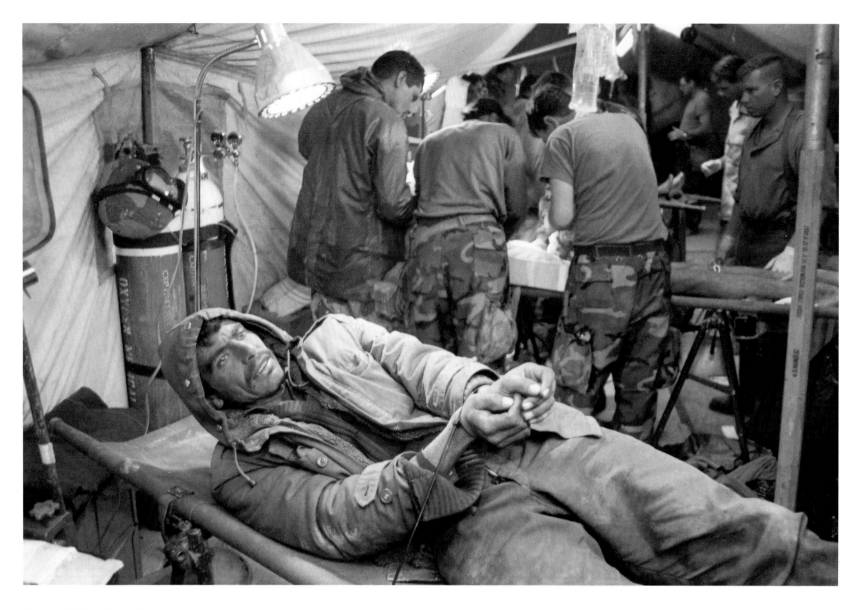

out of bunkers – dancing, skipping, singing with their thumbs up. All some had was white toilet paper to surrender with. Everytime you saw a PoW you were relieved. It was one less guy we would kill or who would kill us.'

Delaney was dismissive of the opposition. On a scale of one to ten, he said, this was one. Most of the time he was more frightened of being killed by his own side, especially the tank-hunting aircraft. Even as the assault began, he had seen US tanks shooting at American lorries by mistake, though luckily no one was killed. Many American troops chose to fight by day because they were so worried about 'friendly fire'. 'We want to fight our fight in the daylight,' said one army divisional commander. The fear of 'friendly' air attack meant helicopters were used more sparingly as they advanced, and

some lead vehicles were given infra-red strobe lights to alert aircraft. But the primary means of identification were little more than an inverted V on the side of the vehicles and an orange sign on the roof.

The problem for the advancing troops was dealing with the dishevelled, under-nourished soldiers who at one time had been called the Prussians of the Middle East. As the Marines pushed forward, they found evidence that far from being a well-organised army, this was closer to a rabble. The deserted bunkers were a clear sign. Those of the ordinary soldiers were pathetically furnished, but Delaney was surprised by the relative luxury of some of the officers' shelters, which resembled Ottoman bordellos with heavy furnishing and pin-up pictures. 'They had taken everything (to the front) – cheap stereos, aerobic exercise books. And

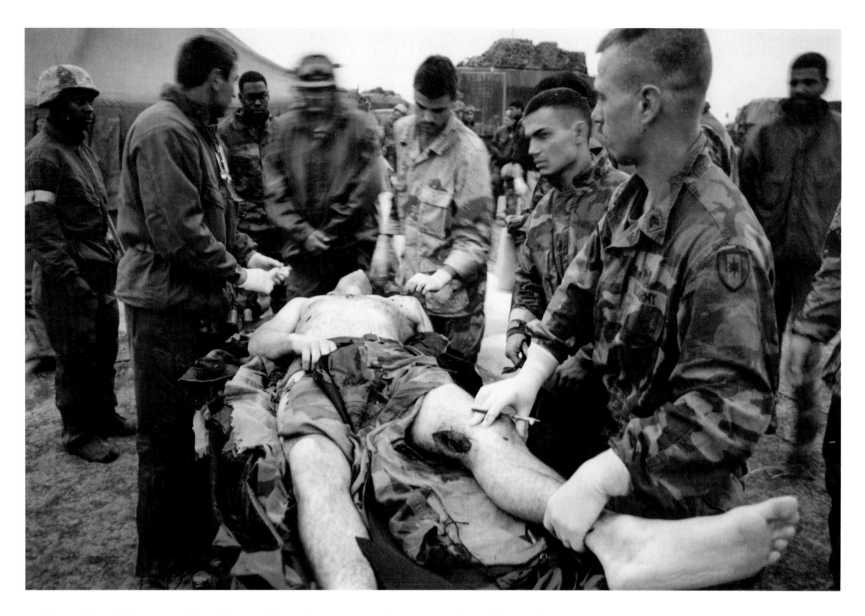

ominous things like women's underwear. It made you wonder what was the story behind it.'

As the Marines sliced with ease into Kuwait in the early hours of February 24, British forces of the 1st Armoured Division, now part of VII Corps, were break-fasting on fried eggs, baked beans and sausages and lis-tening to the BBC World Service. It was reporting that the full assault had started, with Marine and Arab forces invading Kuwait in the east, while far to the west the French Sixth Light Armoured Division and the 82nd Airborne set off 'like a high-speed train' in a headlong rush to seize Salman air base. This was a particular plea-sure to the French; the Americans had only made them redraw their plans once, and the 82nd was the unit which parachuted into Normany at the start of the D-day landings. When General Maurice Schmitt, France's

senior commander, visited US units in the desert, they raised a banner inscribed 'Welcome, General, to Saint-Mère-l'Eglise' (the village behind Omaha beach where the 82nd landed in June, 1944). Even the spirit of Lafayette was summoned from the past to underline this new Franco-American harmony.

The Desert Rats were not due to go in for another twenty-four hours, but the speed of the assault soon changed that. The only delay now was bad weather, which slightly held back the third assault by the 101st Airborne, who intended to 'leapfrog' deep into Iraq. They did manage to leave at 8am on Sunday, however, with hundreds of helicopters surging low over the desert. By the next evening they had seized Highway 8, just 150 miles from Baghdad, from where the brigade commander radioed his HQ: 'Sir,' he said, 'The

An American casualty attended by field medics. In all, 139 Americans were killed in action in the air and land wars. 108 died in accidents leading up to the ground war, more than the number killed in the land battles. The toll compared with 47,000 Americans killed in Vietnam, 264 in Lebanon (1982–4), 18 in Grenada (1983) and 23 in Panama (1989–90) (David Turnley–Detroit Free Press/Colorific)

Iraqi soldiers rush to surrender to American troops. As the allies attacked on February 24, Saddam Hussein exhorted his troops to 'fight them, brave Iraqis', vowing to defeat 'Bush and his stooges.' 'Angels', he said, 'would be at your shoulders'. But all the Iraqis found were M1A1s, Challengers and Apaches on their tails. Hundreds surrendered as soon as the first allied troops appeared, and within a day 10,000 were taken prisoner. Some even killed their commanders who insisted they should fight. By the second day 30,000 had given up and by the end of the war 70,000. Many were to get their first square meal in weeks from allied captors. Though the surrenders slowed the advance, the allies tried to avoid casualties by firing warning rounds at Iraqi positions and sending in psychological warfare teams to broadcast surrender terms in Arabic (Christopher Morris–Black Star/Colorific)

Screaming Eagles have landed in the Euphrates Valley.'

The advance was already going at breathtaking speed, and it encouraged Schwarzkopf to bring forward the timing of the attacks by 'the big boys', the heavy armour. Instead of starting at dawn on Monday, he ordered them to begin their attack at 3pm on Sunday. In a persistent drizzle, the allies began a huge artillery bombardment right along the frontier. The desert shook with the thunder and lightning of the big 155mm guns and the roar of the fearsome Multiple-Launch Rocket Systems (MLRS).

But instead of the expected retaliation, nothing happened. It seemed the Iraqis were overwhelmed. Captured Iraqi commanders were later to confirm the devastation wrought by the artillery. One officer said that of his unit of 250 men only seven remained after being shelled by the MLRS. Another Iraqi officer said that he started the war with 100 guns, which were reduced to eighty by air attacks. After the artillery barrage, however, he had just seven guns. The initial British bombardment had been due to last eighteen hours, but it too was cut short and the charge of the heavy brigades began.

With Union flags fluttering in the breeze, 157 Challenger tanks and 135 Warrior fighting vehicles from Britain's 4th and 7th Armoured Brigades poured through the gaps in the border sand walls blasted open by engineers. There was virtually no resistance. A few tanks put up a fight but were blasted disdainfully aside. Many were facing the wrong direction, still expecting an attack from the south. One Desert Rat described it as similar to a video-game, in which they 'gobbled up Iraqi divisions like Pac-man.'

All along the 300-mile front the Iraqis surrendered in their thousands. Some were so eager to give themselves up that they ran at the troops waving anything vaguely white and shouting 'meals ready to eat', the name for the American ration packs, which they had heard of and presumed to be a gourmet's banquet. In some cases US troops tossed them food, collected their weapons, ran over them with tanks, and pointed the prisoners in the general direction of Saudi Arabia before pushing on.

But mostly they had to round them up and ship them back, slowing the advance. 'It's like a nature hike,' said an American soldier. 'They're jumping up like squirrels to surrender.' One group of three British gunners described how they had been surprised by thirty Iraqis and thought for a terrible moment they were outnumbered. 'Then we realised they were giving themselves up.' Many allied soldiers had to fend off Iraqis intent on kissing them in gratitude. Soldiers soon ran out of plastic flexicuffs to tie prisoners' hands. There were not even enough vehicles to take them back to camps.

American troops capture an Iraqi near Safwan. One man searches him while others keep him covered with pistols (Greg Mathieson–Sipa/Rex)

Opposite: US Marines, who have come under sniper fire, capture an Iraqi suspect (Christoph Simon/AFP)

The desperation to surrender led to some curious incidents. One Iraqi unit tried to hand itself over to a drone – a remote-controlled aircraft that had landed in the desert. Another group put barbed wire around itself and waited patiently until it was found by the allies. In the first twenty-four hours, 10,000 surrendered, by Tuesday it was 30,000. In the end the allies stopped counting. In some cases the prisoners were an asset, pointing out minefields and pinpointing other Iraqi units. Some had been drafted at the last moment, including one American-Iraqi with a Brooklyn accent who said he had been conscripted while visiting his grandmother. 'These guys are mostly farmers, regular people who were forced to join up or have their families killed,' said one US officer. 'They're real nice guys.'

On Monday, the 24th Mechanized Infantry Division, one of the advance units of XVIII Corps, roared into Nasiriyah, where it fought a fierce encounter with an Iraqi commando regiment. The division found hundreds of bunkers full of munitions, weapons, petroleum and other war stocks before thundering down airport runways shooting up the few remaining Iraqi fighter-bombers which had been missed from the air.

After that, they swung down Highway 8 and set about destroying anything in sight, even hitting tanks trying to flee on the back of transporters. As they approached Basra, the Hammurabi Division of the Republican Guard came out to meet them about twenty miles west of the city. There had still been no sign of use of chemical weapons by the Iraqis, but the allied command

Saudi troops take dozens
of Iraqis prisoner inside
Kuwait (Christoph
Simon/AFP)

expected that to change now. Lieutenant General Gary Luck, commander of XVIII Corps, turned to his operations officer, Colonel Frank Akers, and drawled, 'Probably going to get chemmed on this one, Frank.' But they didn't, and at least six Hammurabi battalions were flattened with artillery and rockets. At 3.30am on February 28, the pampered elite troops broke and fled into the dark.

Meanwhile the heavier VII Corps was rolling forward, the pendulum weight behind the left hook. Its commander, Fred Franks, wanted to keep his divisions 'bunched in a big fist'. As a result the Corps moved across a fifty-mile front, 120 miles deep, with hundreds of lorries trailing behind carrying the three million gallons of fuel needed each day. The British 1st Armoured Division was on the left flank, moving with a six-mile front but ready to bunch up to one and a half miles during an attack. The Corps had been alerted that

intercepted signals showed the Iraqis planned to retreat behind a screen of Guards' units, and Schwarzkopf urged it to 'keep pressing, keep pushing.' He didn't need to; the commanders were driving their men on in a headlong cavalry charge.

On Tuesday, as 260,000 soldiers of the two army corps battered their way north, Schwarzkopf ordered them to swing right into Kuwait. One colonel pulled out his maps, studied them for fifteen minutes on the bonnet of his jeep, and then 'cocked his guns and headed east.' Lieutenant General Walter Boomer of the Marines said things were moving so fast that everyone, including himself, was confused. Changing plans were being drawn on cardboard boxes or sketched out in the sand. If it confused the allies, it left the Iraqis in chaos. There was little doubt that they were flabbergasted by the speed of the advance; some were smoking cigarettes or having a meal as the M1A1s and Challengers hit them at

ranges of up to two miles. Several did not have time to get their tanks out from their dug-outs. Everything was moving so fast that it was not unusual for whole units of Iraqi soldiers to be bypassed, or for rearguard allied units to find themselves in the vanguard.

The destruction of the Iraqi army was soon evident in Kuwait City, where thousands of security policemen and soldiers panicked. Grabbing everything they could carry, from looted bottles of scent to television sets, they surged north in stolen vehicles in a mad, desperate rush to escape. Witnesses near the main road recalled the commotion of noise and accidents as the melee sought to leave. On the way they opened fire on Kuwaitis travelling in the opposite direction in a final act of vicious revenge. This extraordinary column, however, got no farther than the Mutlah Gap, near the Iraqi border, where it was discovered by the US Navy's Silverfox squadron.

The squadron had alighted upon the convoy as the planes swooped beneath low cloud cover in the early hours of Tuesday and found itself gazing at a feast of targets – more than 1,500 tanks, armoured vehicles, jeeps, fuel tankers, cars, tractors, and even stolen ambulances and fire engines in a six-lane traffic jam heading north. The bombers fell upon the fleeing Iraqis like wolves.

As the bombs rained down, hundreds of Iraqis abandoned their vehicles and fled into the night, hiding in empty houses and a cemetery. There were so many aircraft trying to get in for the kill that air controllers in the

Left: American soldiers walk past the corpses of half-buried Iraqis as oil wells blaze in the background (Chip Hires–Gamma/FSP)

Above: Men from the Burial Detail, part of the British 4th Armoured Brigade, pick up the remains of Iraqi dead (Mike Moore/*Today*)

American SEAL special forces drive a dune buggy through the outskirts of Kuwait City at night. Lying low during the day, the SEALS (an acronym for sea, air and land) operated by night deep behind enemy lines, harassing Iraqi units. The buggy shown here was specially designed to move fast and quietly (it has a special silencer) over desert terrain. It is armed with a variety of weapons, including a heavy machinegun, grenade launchers and anti-tank weapons.

In all, about 2,000 special forces were deployed in Iraq and Kuwait, including Green Berets, Delta Force, Britain's Special Air Service and French legionnaires. General Schwarzkopf was initially reluctant to use them, but soon valued their work, partially influenced by General De la Billière, a former commander of the SAS. The units undertook many dangerous missions, including searching for Scud missile launchers, kidnapping Iraqi officers, stealing a SAM missile, cutting communciations and using hand-held lasers to illuminate targets for bombers. They also used C-130 planes from which to drop huge 15,000 pound 'daisy cutter' bombs to clear minefields.

The SAS had about 200 men in theatre and favoured a specially-modified open-topped Land-Rover, called the 'Pink Panther', and a new dune buggy, which was carried into Iraq slung beneath Chinook helicopters. The Pink Panther had a three-man crew, and carried two grenade launchers, a 7.62mm machinegun on the dashboard and a 12.7mm Browning on a rear swivel mount. A small satellite navigation system and night vision goggles were included.

One American unit, Task Force 160, rescued downed pilots. Arabic speakers were sent undercover into Kuwait City to contact the resistance and convince the Iraqis that an amphibious landing was imminent. Others dressed as Arabs and drove around in vehicles with Iraqi markings. Schwarzkopf described it as 'a special operations theme park.' At the end of the war 11 Green Berets were missing. One SAS man was killed and seven captured in a battle with Iraqi troops (AFP)

AWACS had to divide air space to prevent collisions. On the aircraft carrier, the USS *Ranger*, pilots were so eager to get back that they had their planes loaded with any available bombs on the flightdeck. The result was one of the most visible slaughters of the war on a road that became known as the 'Highway to Hell'. 'It was bumper to bumper,' said one A6 pilot from the Ranger. 'It was like the road to Daytona Beach at spring break.' Another described the Iraqis as 'sitting ducks'.

The slaughter seemed so random that some in the west who had originally opposed confronting Saddam used it as evidence of a blood-thirsty campaign being fought by the allies. But many of the vehicles were seeking to escape a war zone and would have been able to reinforce the Republican Guard, which was still fighting. Those who died at Mutlah – possibly 200 to 300 – also included some of the most distasteful Iraqis who had helped impose a reign of terror on Kuwait. As one Kuwaiti said after the war, 'they got what they deserved.' A pilot, George Patrick, questioned about what had become known as a 'duck shoot', said 'I think we're past the point of just letting him get in his tanks and drive them back into Iraq and say "I'm sorry".'

By Tuesday night, as the gate slammed shut on Saddam's forces in Kuwait, the elite American and British tank units had already been encountering and defeating units of the Republican Guard. Some of them, such as Tawalkana division, fought hard before they were obliterated, but many seemed nonplussed by the allied strike. Without air cover and with poor communications, they had little chance. Those that tried to flee were trapped by the Shatt al-Arab waterway in the north and Kuwait to the south. Their best hope was to break out through the port of Basra, Iraq's second city. The 24th Mechanised and the 101st and 82nd Airborne units sought to prevent that, and went in hot pursuit. One American colonel, who watched the battle from a helicopter, enthused: 'It's a classic tank-air battle from the textbooks, a tabletop battle.'

For sixteen hours the desert was filled with destruction as the allies hammered the fleeing Iraqis. Tanks were smashing almost everything in sight and a tide of heavy metal left a trail of burning vehicles, bodies and surrendering soldiers. One divisional commander radioed his deputy riding with the forward troops as they took on a unit from the Republican Guard: 'Understand we are engaging the Medina division?' he said. 'Negative, sir,' came the reply. 'We are destroying the Medina division.'

The rout was forcing Saddam's hand. Already on Monday Baghdad radio had announced its forces were being ordered to withdraw, but by then the psychological and military momentum of the advance was too

The Road to Basra. This was all that remained after an attempt by hundreds of Iraqis to escape Kuwait City soon after the start of the land war. Stealing any vehicle they could lay their hands on – including ambulances and fire engines – Iraqis fled the capital under cover of darkness. Apart from the civilian cars and lorries, the desperate rush north included tanks, armoured cars and jeeps. Many of the fleeing Iraqis had been responsible for the brutal repression in Kuwait and were fearful of the consequences as allied forces swept forward to liberate the country.

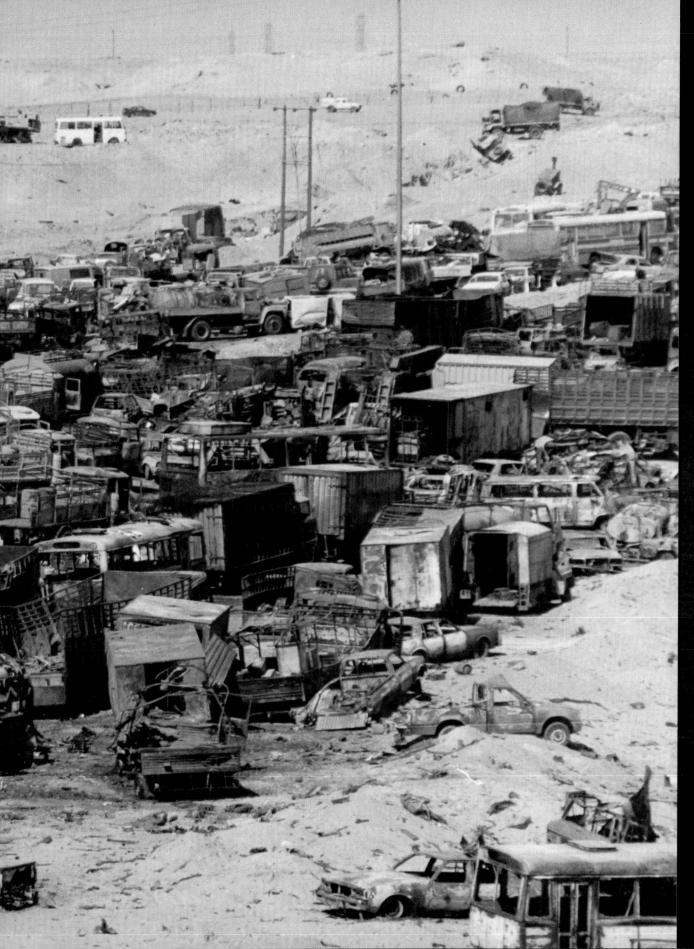

The convoy was spotted by Navy aircraft from the USS *Ranger* in the early hours of February 26. What happened next was described as a 'duck shoot' as hundreds of vehicles were destroyed when allied planes bombed and strafed the road. Journalists at the site estimated the numbers of Iraqis killed at between 200 and 300. The road was soon dubbed the 'Highway to Hell' and led some in the West to question whether the allies were not pursuing a policy of flagrant revenge. Allied commanders pointed out that they were still at war, and these were soldiers fleeing the battle in vehicles that could be used in the conflict. But the publicity played a part in encouraging President Bush to agree to a ceasefire 100 hours after the start of the land war. The decision not to prosecute the war until the Iraqi army was annihilated – as General Schwarzkopf recommended – led to criticism that Bush allowed enough of the army to escape and later ruthlessly suppress uprisings by Shi'ites in the south and Kurds in the north. The plight of the Kurds was to leave a sour taste to the victory celebrations (Mike Moore/*Today*)

great to break off on the say-so of a radio announcer. On Tuesday Saddam made a speech confirming the pull-out, but the Americans demanded more. Bush said he was determined that Saddam, described by the British foreign secretary as a 'bogus, puffed-up frog of a man', should be thoroughly humbled and his army crushed.

By Wednesday the defeat looked complete and the commanders were telling Schwarzkopf that they were running out of things to shoot. Even so, the general said they could carry on, making it a 'battle of annihilation'. But Powell told President Bush that the objective of liberating Kuwait and defeating Saddam had been completed, and that Saddam could claim no kind of victory. He added: 'By tonight there won't be an enemy left.' Bush, not wishing to be accused of mindless slaughter and conscious of staying within the United Nations' resolutions, gathered his war cabinet and told them: 'I want to stop the killing.' He also wanted terms for a permanent ceasefire agreed within two days with Iraqi commanders. One aide pointed out that a ceasefire at midnight Washington time would mean the war had lasted 100 hours. It was a nice, round figure, and Bush agreed to end the war then.

At 3.30am local time on Thursday, divisional commanders were told to prepare for a temporary ceasefire at 8am. The fighting went on for the rest of the night, with helicopters attacking the retreating Iraqis, but it was all but over, bar a couple of sporadic engagements over the next few days. The ceasefire, however, did mean that 700 tanks, including hundreds of T-72s from

Left: British engineers flying the skull and crossbones approach the road to Basra on February 30, four days after the Iraqi convoy had been bombed by US Navy planes. The men, from the Royal Engineers, called themselves the 'Graves Commission', saying their job was to bury the dead and clear the wreckage from the highway. As they approached, the engines of several vehicles were still running; unexploded bombs were also detonating. The smoke in the background was from one such explosion. The task of clearing the road proved highly dangerous as large numbers of unexploded cluster bombs still littered the area (Ken Lennox/*Daily Mirror*)

Above: The remains of an Iraqi horribly burnt during the air raids on the road to Basra (Kenneth Jarecke–Contact/Colorific)

the Republican Guard, and 1,400 armoured personnel carriers escaped the rout.

That aside, the mood among the fighting men was ecstatic. They could not believe it had been so easy and their own losses so light. 'We killed 630 tanks and only lost four tanks and two Bradleys,' said General Ronald Griffith, commander of the 1st Division. 'It was most probably the most powerful armoured division on the move in history. This is going to go down as one of the great armoured campaigns.' About 3,850 Iraqi tanks had been destroyed in the AirLand battle, far more than the 2,700 German tanks lost in the battle for Kursk in 1943, regarded as one of the greatest tank battles.

Soldiers scampered around the desert waving their national flags and posing for pictures beside wrecked Iraqi tanks. One American unit blasted James Brown over loud speakers singing 'I feel good'. Others sat dazed, baffled that it was all over so fast. Brigadier Patrick Cordingley, commander of the British 7th Armoured Brigade, said 'it was a time of great exhilaration, mixed with the awfulness of coming across so many bodies in cold blood, so to speak, and seeing their tanks and vehicles smashed to bits. Remember, very few of us had ever experienced combat, let alone on this scale.' Sir Peter de la Billière, a former Special Air Service commander who had seen as much action in his career as Schwarzkopf, described the allied triumph as 'perhaps one of the greatest victories that we've ever experienced, certainly in our lives and possibly in history. Get out there and ring your church bells.'

Once the heat of battle had cooled, however, the allies began to reassess the conflict. It was true that the attack had gone almost faultlessly. It had destroyed the shibboleth that attackers needed a three to one advantage and it had changed the view that air power could not win wars. As they gazed at the havoc wreaked by the bombers and the endless lines of prisoners, it was evident that the morale of the Iraqis had been broken from the air. However well they might have performed in defence against the Iranians in their eight-year war of attrition, they were not in the same league as the United States. The allies were looking at a shattered Third World army.

But while much had gone right, there were some worrying discoveries. Intelligence had been accurate in parts, but it had got some things wrong, which against a more determined and skilled foe might have proved dangerous. One was the extent of Iraqi defences. Minefields meant to be 2,000 yards deep turned out to be only 140 yards wide; 'huge' oil-filled trenches were only a couple of yards wide; the berms were pathetic, and underground bunkers were lined with corrugated iron and two layers of sandbags, too thin to stop a

US Marines after the land battle head off to inspect a burning Iraqi tank (Bruno Barbey/Magnum)

mortar round. Even intelligence assessments of the Iraqis themselves appeared inflated. Some Americans had expected to find great hulking soldiers. They were surprised when they encountered waiflike men desperate to surrender. Some felt cheated; this was hardly a worthy enemy, they said.

Most baffling, however, was the absence of chemical weapons. The allies had 'categorical' evidence that Saddam intended to use them. Though some artillery rounds were found which had been painted yellow (a warning sign of poison gas), none was fired. Nor were any chemical weapons actually discovered, despite an intensive search. William Webster, director of the CIA, had told Congress before the war that Iraq had stockpiled 1,000 tons of nerve gas and other variants of mass destruction. If so, where were they? The only conclusion reached by the allied commanders was that Saddam did not have time to transport them to front-line troops. But that conflicted with signals' intelligence that commanders had been given authority to use chemical weapons at will. One possible explanation was that they were held back because their shelf-life was limited, and the intention had been to distribute them on the eve of war. Another was that Saddam feared chemical retaliation. Given his utter disregard for the lives of his men, that seemed unlikely. In the end the commanders had to admit they did not know why they had not been 'slimed', and could only be grateful.

The ease of victory led to instant judgments, almost a downplaying of the achievement. General Boomer of the Marines said that 'while we should be proud of what we have done, I don't think it's wise to get a big head about this war. I wouldn't want people to think that every war that you find yourself in would turn out to be quite as easy as this one.' Most Americans, however, were happy to revel in the triumph. Though the British could look back on their defeat of Argentina in the Falklands in 1982, the United States had not had a clean-cut victory like this since V-J day in 1945, when its new heroes, Schwarzkopf and Powell, were aged ten and eight. Now it indulged itself in a bout of patriotic pride, and forgot the humiliations that had occasionally accompanied its role as a superpower.

Nor was the victory quite as easy as Boomer implied. The Iraqis had once been a formidable force, and most of the allies were far from home, with long supply lines. The combined AirLand battle was well conceived and brilliantly executed. If Schwarzkopf was looking for a place in military history, he had found it. Just as he studied Hannibal's and Montgomery's triumphs, future generations at military academies will pore over the plans of Schwarzkopf's 100 Hour War and marvel at how simple it all looked.

LIBERATION

commander whose troops had just fought a bloody battle for control of the international airport, rode into town on top of a troop carrier. 'Makes you appreciate freedom, doesn't it?' he drawled.

The troops had entered the city in a rush as reports began to filter out during the land war of further atrocities as the Iraqis exacted their final acts of revenge. The reports turned out to be true. The city's morgue had forty-one corpses with bullet, knife and burn wounds, many with their eyes gouged out. But that was only the most visible evidence. At a suburban cemetery in the Riqqa district, gravediggers claimed about three quarters of the 1,000 corpses buried there had been shot. Torture chambers were uncovered with the electrodes still plugged into the mains sockets and ghastly pin-ups still stuck on the walls. Even the zoo animals had not escaped this tide of malevolence; many had been eaten or starved. Once again the relentless tales of torture and pillage, of children being shot and women raped and murdered, assailed the ears of the allies. Everyone had a horror story and many were in a state of shock.

'What the Iraqis did was beyond belief,' one Kuwaiti doctor said. The British ambassador, Michael Weston, who soon returned to the embassy where he had eked out his miserable existence under the Iraqi siege, said the word 'barbaric' was inadequate to describe their behaviour. What sort of people could have done this, the Kuwaitis demanded? It was as bad, if not worse, than the stories brought out by fleeing exiles.

Saddam had left other things to remember him by. Never one to be magnanimous in defeat, he scorched the earth, literally. More than 600 oil wells were blown up, the flaming beacons and dark skies a reminder that if he could not enjoy the underground riches of Kuwait, nor could its people. The beaches, too, where Kuwaitis had strolled alongside the Gulf waters, now looked like Normandy after D-Day. They were littered with barbed wire and unexploded mines and ammunition which had already begun to take a toll of small, playful children. But at least the city had been spared the havoc that would have accompanied a battle for the capital. It was true that some houses had been razed in the struggle to eliminate the resistance, and other buildngs had been destroyed - including the parliament, national museum, hotels, government offices and the emir's Dasman Palace. But much of the city was intact. It was the scar of occupation, though, which rankled most. 'We will never forget them,' said one young Kuwaiti. 'It will be like the Jews and Germans.'

There was a tangible mood of revenge. Allied forces and resistance fighters were carefully screening Iraqi prisoners to find those responsible for the atrocities, but it was not an easy task. Many of the worst offenders had

ON 27 February, 1991, six months and twenty-five days after the Iraqis parked their tanks on the corniche and drove the emir from power, another column of armoured vehicles clattered into Kuwait City. Like the Iraqis, the advancing troops were greeted with gunfire, but this time it was the chatter of Kalashnikovs being fired by resistance fighters in wild celebration. 'Alahu Akbar' cried the people of the capital at the grinning Kuwaiti and Saudi liberators. American Marines were greeted with cries of 'USA, USA' and 'we love you' as normally demure young Kuwaiti women kissed the conquering soldiers.

The euphoric scenes were set against a tragic backdrop; a sky turned black by hundreds of blazing oil wells, and a once-proud, gleaming city reduced to desolation, with not even water or electricity to provide the basics of modern life. Many of its inhabitants had fled, and in the last days of the war the Iraqis had dragged thousands more back to Basra. But for a few joyous days the misery of occupation was forgotten. Everywhere the Kuwaiti flag was held aloft; one child was wrapped in a national flag and held up to be hugged by soldiers. Lieutenant General Walter Boomer, the Marine

fled and much of the evidence had been destroyed. Some of the main culprits – the Mukhabarat and the military secret police – were found and dragged off to uncertain fates. But, as in Paris after the 1944 liberation, much of the hatred was reserved for collaborators, real or not.

The Palestinians, of whom there had been about 400,000 before the invasion, were regarded as the main culprits. The resistance claimed that about 50,000 of the 180,000 who had remained through the occupation had assisted the Iraqis in one form or another. This was vehemently denied by the Palestinians, but there was little doubt that the Iraqis regarded them as tacit allies, largely because of the support for Saddam from Yasser Arafat's PLO. The Iraqis, too, were able to feed on Palestinian resentment of Kuwaitis for refusing them citizenship, even though many had been born in Kuwait.

As a result some did assist the invaders, pointing out resistance members and helping at road blocks. In return, they were given minor privileges. But many remained neutral, and a small handful even aided the resistance. All that was forgotten, though, in the scramble for revenge. Many of the most vengeful were those Kuwaitis who had fled the country, more so than those who had stayed and seen events at first hand. One of them spoke before his return of giving the Palestinians 'another Sabra and Shatila', a reference to the camps where hundreds of Palestinians were murdered in Beirut after the Israeli invasion of 1982. In the Hawli district, graffiti appeared saying: 'Death to the Palestinians traitors. We don't want them.'

Gangs of armed Kuwaitis took the law into their own hands, hunting down any Palestinian suspected of even remotely collaborating. One Palestinian woman said her three sons were blindfolded, beaten and taken away to a police station. She had not seen them since, and did not know their fate. Bodies turned up, some of them with cigarette burns and other signs of torture. There were reports of hundreds of Palestinians disappearing. But the evidence was murky, and the city was gripped by rumour and fear. Others began to flee, fearing a pogrom. More thoughtful Kuwaitis, and the American and British troops who had helped liberate the country, became uncomfortably aware that there was little to distinguish this behaviour from that of the Iraqis. The government, such as it was, seemed helpless. 'If (such incidents) are confirmed,' said the minister of planning, Suleiman al-Mutawa, 'we ought to be ashamed.'

The al-Sabahs, however, had a monumental task. The crown prince returned soon after the liberation to take control of a situation that was spiralling out of control. He sought to impose some form of order by authorising a three-month period of martial law and gave the police

American special forces join in the celebrations. They played a key role in the liberation, acting as liaison officers with Saudi and Kuwaiti units and helping clear and protect the US embassy (Saussier– Gamma/FSP)

greater authority. But almost everyone was armed, and while scores were being settled there was little the authorities could do short of a military crackdown. The government, however, was unimpressive. Despite having seven months to plan its return and the restoration of emergency services, it was seized by indecision and torpor. It took many weeks for even basic supplies to resume, and in the meantime resentment grew.

Part of the problem was that the water pumping and electricity generating stations had been destroyed. It required skilled labour to get them working again, and that in turn meant employing Palestinians, who were largely responsible for keeping Kuwait going before the invasion. Many had now fled or were too intimidated to work, so the situation got no better. The distribution of emergency food supplies, too, was poorly handled, much of it held up by unnecessary bureaucracy and a determination to prevent foreigners getting access. Even the Kuwaitis began to point out that the city worked better under the Iraqis.

It soon became evident, however, that the government-in-exile had at least reached one decision: to reshape the demographic form of the nation. They were painfully aware not only of their failure to defend the country, but of how Kuwaitis were a minority in their own land. The plan was to deport foreigners or refuse re-entry to those who had fled. Before the invasion the population was about two million, with 700,000 Kuwaitis. The al-Sabahs wanted a million of those removed, making Kuwaitis the majority. It was decided that any problems caused by such a drastic reduction in the population could be met by more high-technology industries, by Kuwaitis doing more for themselves and employing fewer servants, and by construction contracts being completed with short-term labour. 'This is a God-sent opportunity to upgrade and modernise our whole system,' said Abdul Latif al-Hamad, the former finance minister. 'This is our chance.'

Others, however, saw it as a chance for something far more distasteful to the al-Sabahs; a form of democracy.

Though the ruling family had dabbled with an ersatz democracy, they were clearly not proponents of universal suffrage. A 1962 constitution, which excluded women and 'second grade' Kuwaitis from the vote, had permitted a parliament made up of elected representatives and nominees. It had been suspended in 1986 when it became too critical. Now there were calls for full democratic reforms, which were receiving tacit support from the allies.

The demands had already raised the political temperature, and stories were circulating of how the al-Sabahs had hired hit squads to exact revenge against opposition leaders. One pro-democracy figure, Hamed al-Jouaan, just survived after he was shot at his door by unknown assailants. 'After what we've been through,' he proclaimed from his hospital bed, 'the people are ready to fight for their rights.' The emir, who had attracted criticism for his tardy return, eventually came back on March 14 once the gold taps had been installed in his temporary palace. He attempted to defuse the tension by

promising greater democracy, including the vote for women, when the crisis of reconstruction had been overcome; meanwhile his cabinet resigned in recognition of its failure to restore services.

The political convulsions aside, the emir's most pressing problem was ending the oil fires and rebuilding the country. Not only were the blazing oil wells an environmental hazard, but they were devouring tens of millions of dollars a day that could be used in reconstruction. Texan oil cappers, from companies called Wild Well Control or Boots and Coots, were soon striding around the landscape in stetsons, shaking their heads. Even Red Adair, the legendary firefighter, said that he had 'never seen anything like this before.' But trouble meant cash, and everywhere international companies were rushing to get contracts to rebuild the palaces, airports, hospitals and refineries. Conservative estimates reckoned it would cost £100 billion to restore the country to its former opulence.

In the West, there were other problems that came with

General Norman Schwarzkopf escorts Lieutenant General Sultan Hashim Ahmed (third from right) and other senior Iraqi officers to a tent to sign the terms for a ceasefire on 3 March, 1991. The meeting took place at an airbase on the Iraqi-Kuwaiti border. It imposed tough conditions on the Iraqis, which they were forced to accept. A permanent ceasefire was only agreed at the United Nations on April 9, after the Iraqis had inflicted a terrible defeat on rebellious Kurds in the north and forced millions to flee (Greg Gibson/AP)

BRITISH EMBASSY

COMMERCIAL AND ADMINISTRATION SECTIONS

OPEN TO THE PUBLIC SATURDAY TO WEDNESDAY

Far left:Two Kuwaitis wander through the streets of the abandoned city carrying pictures of the emir. The devastation, though serious, could have been worse. Though several buildings were set on fire, most of the city remained intact. The Iraqis, however, did leave large numbers of munitions lying around, which claimed many lives among children. Most of the damage inflicted on the Kuwaitis was psychological, caused by casual brutality and the systematic use of torture against suspected members of the resistance, which remained active throughout the occupation. The allies found the city littered with looted belongings that the Iraqis did not have time to transport home. But during the seven-month occupation they managed to plunder the most valuable treasures of the immensely-rich emirate (Gilles Bassignac–Gamma/FSP)

Left: A Sea King helicopter lowers special forces into the empty British embassy in Kuwait City on February 28 to check for booby traps before the return of the ambassador, Michael Weston. The troops used stun grenades to clear rooms in the building, which they feared might be occupied by Iraqi troops who had refused to accept the ceasefire, and explosives to blow off doors. Weston, who had lived in the embassy on basic rations until mid-December, arrived soon afterwards. His first act was to replace the tattered Union flag – which had flown over the embassy throughout the occupation – with a new one. Another of his tasks was to locate the 30-odd Britons who had stayed throughout the occupation. Most were either Arabs with British passports, or were married to Kuwaitis. (Steve Back/Daily Mail)

Above: Relatives undertake the grisly task of looking for bodies at a morgue in Kuwait City. Stories about Iraqi atrocities had been filtering out of Kuwait for months, but it was only after the liberation that the true extent of the horror became known. Torture chambers were found and almost every Kuwaiti had a story about how they had been maltreated, or how relatives and friends had been tortured or had disappeared. Some of the crimes were horrific; the Iraqis had resorted to electrocution and mutilation of Kuwaitis for minor offences or for ill-found suspicions that they were members of the resistance. Corpses were founded with their eyes gouged out and with holes drilled with electric power tools (Van der Stockt–Gamma/FSP)

A Kuwaiti resistance fighter drags a Palestinian suspected of collaboration away for interrogation. After the liberation many Kuwaitis, and especially those who had been abroad during the occupation, exacted revenge on the Palestinian community, which until then had been the hewers of wood and drawers of oil. The government failed to intervene; many Kuwaitis were heavily armed, setting up rival militias to the police and army. Even though the vast majority of Palestinians stayed neutral during the Iraqi occupation, some did assist the Iraqis, largely out of resentment against Kuwaitis who had refused them citizenship. This was enough to lead to a general witch-hunt, with people being dragged off on fragile pretexts. Many Palestinians were tortured, and several bodies turned up after summary executions. Western diplomats expressed alarm that there was little to distinguish this behaviour from that of the Iraqis. The persecution led to an exodus of Palestinians from the country, and the Kuwaitis made it clear that they would cut drastically the numbers of foreigners, allowing Kuwaiti nationals to become the majority (Christopher Morris–Black Star/Colorific)

the peace. Having survived the war, Saddam was able ruthlessly to suppress internal rebellions by the Kurds in the north and the Shi'ites in the south. That raised the questions about whether the allies should have carried on to prise him from his network of bunkers in Baghdad and put him on trial for war crimes. Bush came under fire for not moving fast enough to help the friendless Kurds as they scampered up the Anatolian mountains to escape the helicopter gunships and tanks of what was left of the Iraqi army. It was a difficult time for the president, who until then had handled the crisis with all the inarticulate yet accomplished aplomb of an old-fashioned Yankee familiar with the ways of the world. He had stopped the war because he did not want America to become embroiled in such a volatile region, and because the public mood was swinging against the killing. It was a nice, swift victory; why spoil it by getting too involved?

But the war meant that America was now far more involved in the region than it had ever been. Even before the first shots of the war had been fired, the Pentagon and State Department were planning the post-war Middle East world. They accepted now that the United States would have to play a much more active role in the region and pre-position weaponry and troops there. But they were also wary of the problems. James Baker, long reluctant to get involved, warned that 'modern history has shown that no single nation can impose its will or remake the Middle East in its image.'

His colleagues in the Washington power structure were even more reluctant to accept a wider role, that America should become 'Globo-Cop' policing the world against small-time dictators. But Bush has other ideas. He told Congress on 5 March, 1991, that the Gulf war was the 'first test of a new world coming into view, a world in which there is the very real prospect of a new world order.' It was vague, but the cynics thought they knew what he meant; a world order in which the super-power struggle had ended and in which nasty dictators did what they were told by the United States. In 1988, at his nomination acceptance speech, Bush had told his audience: 'We saved Europe, cured polio, went to the moon and lit the world with our culture. Now we are on the verge of a new century, and what country's name will it bear? I say it will be another American century.' At least Bush could now say that he had struck a blow for freedom everywhere by forcing an invader to retreat. It had reinforced the inviolability of frontiers, and no doubt deterred a few who had coveted their neighbours' land. It had restored America's confidence and showed that the end of the Cold War could bring other benefits. But the problem, as ever, once the war had been won, was winning the peace.

A US soldier returns to McGuire air force base in New Jersey. All the allied troops were determined to get out of the Gulf as soon as possible once the war was over. Units from the 82nd Airborne had been in the desert since August, 1990. When politicians visited the troops, the most frequent question was, 'When are you going to get us out of here?' Part of the reason for President Bush refusing to prosecute the war to bring about the overthrow of Saddam Hussein was that he did not want to keep his troops in the Gulf any longer. Domestic pressure in the United States wanted a quick victory and a quick return. Soon after the liberation, the Americans announced that they were accelerating the pull-out to 5,000 troops a day. Six weeks after the end of the war, they had already withdrawn more than 200,000 soldiers (Nina Berman–Sipa/Rex)

Opposite: Two girls hold a picture of their father, Specialist Frederick McCallum of the 24th Mechanised Infantry Division, at Hunter's air force base, Georgia, just before his return (Tony Savino–Sipa/Rex)

Overleaf: The legacy of Saddam Hussein. Not even the camels escaped his brutal occupation (Bruno Barbey/Magnum)

188

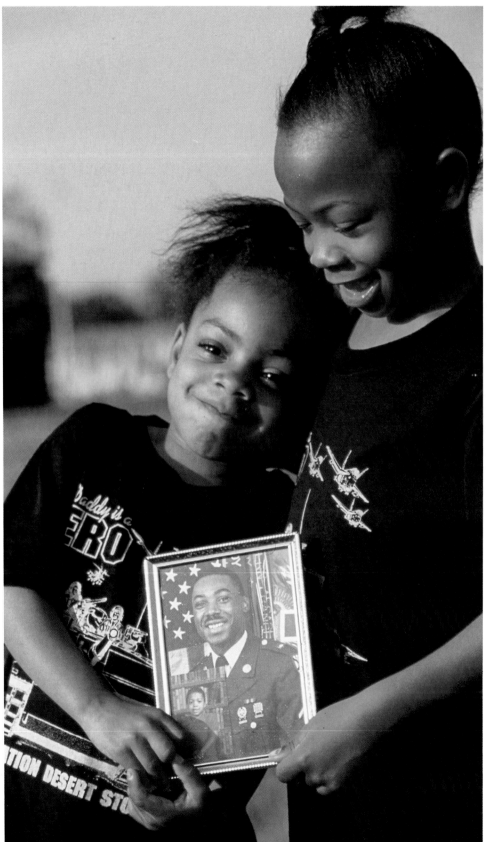